# the sentence book

# the sentence book

### LEE A. JACOBUS

University of Connecticut

**HARCOURT BRACE JOVANOVICH, INC.**

New York     Chicago     San Francisco     Atlanta

ISBN: 0-15-579640-2

Library of Congress Catalog Card Number: 75-32466

Printed in the United States of America

# preface

*The Sentence Book* developed in response to a need for brief, direct instruction in writing strong sentences. It does not impose unfamiliar and difficult concepts on student or instructor but builds on traditional approaches to the sentence. The strengths of this presentation are its simplicity, its ease of use, its flexibility, and its step-by-step handling of such basic functions as coordination and subordination.

Good writers often reveal their skill through subordination, since subordination modifies ideas and places them in relationship to central concepts. In this book, treatment of the principles of subordination follows a careful discussion of the principles of coordination. Each concept is crucial for writers and each must be handled well if a writer is to compose good sentences; the progressive presentation of the two makes them both easier to grasp.

The elements of the sentence are taken up one at a time, with each subsequent unit offering alternatives for building sentences that clarify relationships between ideas. Familiar problems, like the sentence fragment, the run-on sentence, pronoun-and-verb agreement, are all treated in individual units. Once the basic elements have been worked through, students should be ready to go on to some of the traditional rhetorical devices writers have used to affect their audiences. Variation of sentence length and structure, parallel construction, the imperative and direct address, and other basic rhetorical modes are introduced and illustrated in the final two sections of the book.

Most basic punctuation problems are also treated; they are presented as Punctuation Pointers, which appear as they are needed rather than in isolated units. For example, the punctuation of coordinate clauses, introductory subordinate elements, and introductory participial phrases is explained when these elements are introduced in a full discussion. Punctuation is taught when it is pertinent, making it more likely to be used properly.

Punctuation Pointers are supplemented by Composition Pointers, which provide opportunities for students to examine their own writing for examples of the constructions each unit discusses. The Composition Pointers give students a chance to apply what they have learned. This approach emphasizes an important point: *The Sentence Book* is designed to produce real improvement in writing, not skill in filling in blanks. The book is for writers, and what it teaches is writing.

In using the book, students should start with the first unit that gives them some difficulty. They should then progress unit by unit through the rest of the book, reviewing earlier material where necessary. The student writer is most likely to benefit from covering every unit from the beginning to the end of the text, because the book stresses the importance of starting from a central core—the simple subject—and building around it. The coherence that such an approach provides depends on an understanding of basic principles as they are presented, and helps the writer clarify ideas before the act of writing itself.

The book is designed to be used in a classroom with an instructor who can go over specific points and reinforce important concepts. However, its progressive nature helps make the book self-instructional. Since most writers will know when they have difficulty with a given unit, they can request help as they need it. Instructors responding to such requests may find that trouble spots will become apparent if students are asked to read instructions and descriptions in a given unit aloud. Listening to students read important passages can often help uncover any source of misunderstanding.

Three tests are supplied at the end of the book. The first is a brief diagnostic test that examines the student's knowledge of the simple subject and predicate verb, the sentence fragment, and agreement; a writing sample is also asked for. This pretest should reveal serious writing problems. The second test is keyed to the eight units of Section I, the basic elements of the sentence; and the third test to Section II, the clause and the phrase. The questions in these two tests are designed to explore specific areas in which problems may arise or persist.

These tests may be used in any of several ways. They can all be used as diagnostic tests to determine at what point in the text individual students should begin. They can also serve as achievement tests, or posttests, to be administered after the text material has been studied; they can be given unit by unit or section by section. Finally, some instructors may wish to use the tests as both diagnostic and achievement evaluators; as long as there is at least a two-week time lapse, the tests may be used in both ways.

For units that may give individual students special problems, the tests may also provide supplemental examples. If, for instance, during a lesson on the sentence fragment, an instructor finds that more examples are needed, he or she may wish to use the test material to augment the text. In this case, the "tests" become more important as instructional tools than as evaluative ones.

Many more people contributed to this book than can be acknowledged. The students in the University of Connecticut Summer Program inspired the book. Rufus Blanshard in the Cameroons lent a critical and profitably skeptical eye to the development of the original version. Sean Golden, Notre Dame University; Sharon Johnson, Hampshire College; Linnell Nesmith, Hartford High School; Arnold Orza, University of Connecticut—Hartford; Betsy Clark, University of Connecticut—Storrs; Luis Perez-Cordero, Eastern Connecticut State College; Donald B. Gibson, Rutgers University; and Robert Miles, Sacramento State University, all contributed time and effort to early and late stages of the manuscript. Madge Manfred of Mohegan Community College gave the manuscript a valuable critical reading. I am grateful to all these readers and to all those others who in one way or another helped to make this a better book.

LEE A. JACOBUS

# contents

SECTION

## II

Constructing Clauses and Phrases  53

SECTION

III

Principles of Coordination        81

SECTION

Principles of Subordination　　99

SECTION

# VII

## Tests and Evaluations    185

the sentence book

# basic parts
# and
# basic problems

# The Simple Subject

Every complete sentence has at least two parts: the simple subject and the simple predicate. The simple subject can be the single word or words which name the main person, place, thing, or idea of the sentence. Usually we find the subject in the beginning of the sentence rather than at the end. Therefore most sentences we write and speak look like this:

This pattern is basic to English speech and English writing and should be mastered quickly.

**The proper name**

The subject is the name of something. Therefore any proper name, such as those which follow, can be the subject of a sentence:

| | |
|---|---|
| 1. Zaida | 6. Edward Lewis Wallant |
| 2. Billy the Kid | 7. Uncle Paul |
| 3. Rita | 8. Harold Wilson |
| 4. Reggie Jackson | 9. Mary Pickford |
| 5. Kenneth Galbraith | 10. Kareem Abdul Jabbar |

The name of any person can be the subject of a sentence. In the following spaces write the names of five of your friends. Then write the names of five people you have heard of, but whom you do not know personally.

1. _____    4. _____

2. _____    5. _____

3. _____    6. _____

7. _____   9. _____

8. _____   10. _____

There are other kinds of names that can serve as the simple subject of a sentence. The next list gives names of movies, buildings, books, TV shows, businesses, and institutions.

1. *The Sting*
2. *Gone with the Wind*
3. *A Raisin in the Sun*
4. The Paramount Theater
5. The Hollywood Bowl
6. Shea Stadium
7. *Down These Mean Streets*
8. *The Great Gatsby*
9. *Guinness Book of Records*
10. *Shaft*
11. *The Carol Burnett Show*
12. *Face the Nation*
13. Aetna Life Insurance Company
14. The Bank of America
15. Polaroid Corporation
16. Manchester Community College
17. The United Nations
18. Boy Scouts of America

---

**PUNCTUATION POINTER**

The examples above show that the first letter of each word of a proper name is capitalized. The shorter words in a title, such as "in" or "the," are not capitalized unless they come first. The names of books, films, and TV shows are in italics, as *The Sting*. When typing or writing such a name, use underlining to stand for italics, as in this example: The Sting.

---

In the following spaces give the proper names of any movies, TV shows, buildings, places, businesses, schools, or institutions you have heard about.

1. _____   5. _____

2. _____   6. _____

3. _____   7. _____

4. _____   8. _____

9. _____    15. _____

10. _____    16. _____

11. _____    17. _____

12. _____    18. _____

13. _____    19. _____

14. _____    20. _____

Now take a minute to see if you have used capitals where they are needed and have underlined the names of books, movies, or TV shows.

## Abstract ideas

All the proper names above are given to people, places, or things which can be, more or less, seen or heard. Even businesses are in a given place and hire workers who work in buildings with the business name on them. But when we describe things that cannot be seen or heard or in any way observed directly by our five senses, we describe something which is abstract. The word "abstract" only means that we are talking about something that can be thought of or felt emotionally, but that cannot be seen in the way we can see a person. Yet even abstract things, such as human emotions, can be simple subjects, and in turn can be part of a sentence. Next is a list of emotions we can feel.

1. love          6. surprise
2. irritation    7. fright
3. nervousness   8. coolness
4. excitement    9. hesitancy
5. hate         10. envy

None of these are concrete or touchable. We can see what these emotions do to people, but we can't see the emotions themselves. Therefore we must call them abstract. Make a list below of emotions you have felt yourself. Do not use any from the list above.

1. _____    6. _____

2. _____    7. _____

3. _____    8. _____

4. _____    9. _____

5. _____    10. _____

Some ideas are not emotions, yet they are abstract. They, too, can be simple subjects and part of a sentence. Most of these words describe a condition of people or things. These are not emotions.

| | | |
|---|---|---|
| 1. poverty | 8. determination | 15. piracy |
| 2. hunger | 9. privacy | 16. colonialism |
| 3. freedom | 10. courtesy | 17. seriousness |
| 4. independence | 11. diplomacy | 18. unconcern |
| 5. aggressiveness | 12. cleverness | 19. artistry |
| 6. ambition | 13. ignorance | 20. destruction |
| 7. awareness | 14. nonsense | |

Below, write your own list of abstract words which can be used as simple subjects. Avoid using a word which is also the name of an emotion. Find words which name or describe the conditions of people, places, or things.

1. _____    4. _____

2. _____    5. _____

3. _____    6. _____

7. _____   9. _____

8. _____   10. _____

## Common names

Finally, there are many names of things and activities which are not abstract and not proper names. A proper name is proper to only one person or thing, such as Ralph Ellison—it is the name of a specific man, not a general group of men. Ellison is a writer, and the word "writer" is a common name, since it is a name given to many people. The list which follows offers some common names, which can all be simple subjects in a sentence.

| | |
|---|---|
| 1. cowboys | 11. beginnings |
| 2. stairs | 12. insults |
| 3. manifold | 13. joke |
| 4. bass guitar | 14. information |
| 5. playing | 15. remarks |
| 6. postage stamp | 16. newspapers |
| 7. running | 17. racing |
| 8. mountains | 18. passageway |
| 9. riffs | 19. movies |
| 10. stories | 20. whispering |

Add your own common names in the spaces provided below. Be sure each is the name of a thing or activity you can see, hear, taste, touch, or smell, and that it is not a name which is given only to a single person or thing.

---

**PUNCTUATION POINTER**

The common name does not need a capital letter at its beginning because it names a general class of things. It also never needs underlining (italics) or quotation marks to identify it. Again, this is because, unlike the proper name, the common name is of a general group of things. The words you list below, then, need no special punctuation.

---

1. _____   3. _____

2. _____   4. _____

5. _____    13. _____

6. _____    14. _____

7. _____    15. _____

8. _____    16. _____

9. _____    17. _____

10. _____    18. _____

11. _____    19. _____

12. _____    20. _____

# The Subject with Completers

Most of the sentences we speak or write do not have simple subjects. They have subjects which use words or groups of words to make a fuller statement. We use many kinds of completers but we need not name each kind. The pattern below shows the general way in which we can make a simple subject more complete in meaning. The basic method is to add words which describe, make clear, or somehow limit the meaning of the simple subject.

> simple subject:   the woman
> completer:   upstairs
> simple subject with completer:   the woman upstairs

The completer word helps identify the woman in question. If there are a great many women upstairs, we might have to be more exact. If the woman we mean lives in Apartment C, we might have a subject with completers that looks like this:

> the woman upstairs in Apartment C

Now the completers make the simple subject much more clearly identified.

Completers do not always come right after the simple subject. For instance, the following pattern is quite common:

> simple subject:   friend
> completer:   my
> simple subject with completer:   my friend

Consider the following variations on this pattern, and notice how much more exact we can be in each example:

> 1. my best friend
> 2. my only true friend
> 3. my only true male friend

Of course it is almost possible to continue forever. We could add a completer to the end of this expression to make it even more exact:

> 4. my only true male friend from back home

Each time we add a completer that tells us who, where, when, how, why, or what, we describe the simple subject more fully.

The examples below show a number of basic patterns we can use in developing the simple subject. In each case the completers make the subject more clear, more exact in meaning. But note very carefully: the completers do not make the subject do anything. This is extremely important because once the subject is put into action, we are not building a subject with completers; we are building a sentence. All the following examples have the simple subject underlined. Each example is that of a simple subject with completers. In each case ask yourself what the completer does. What does it add to your knowledge of the simple subject?

1. <u>Linda Jenkins</u> from security
2. <u>Jasper</u>, the fellow running for president,
3. <u>Zaida's friend</u> with the Toronado
4. last at bat but first on base, <u>Reggie Jackson</u>,
5. <u>Edward Lewis Wallant</u>, the <u>writer</u>,
6. <u>Mary Pickford</u>, silent film star,
7. everyone's <u>happiness</u>

8. unpleasant <u>memories</u>
9. <u>Kareem Abdul Jabbar</u>, high scorer,
10. <u>Erskine Childers</u>, Ireland's former President,

**PUNCTUATION POINTER**

When the completer expresses an idea which *is* the subject, we set that completer off with commas. The technical term for this is apposition. Phrases and clauses used in apposition need commas. In example 9 above, there is only one high scorer, Kareem Abdul Jabbar. Therefore we could say that example 9 might be described in this way:

| Kareem Abdul Jabbar | = | high scorer |
|---|---|---|

This is the case in examples 2, 4, 5, 6, 9, and 10 above. Such completers, in clarifying the simple subject, actually restate or equal the subject.

Completers always add descriptive information to the simple subject or identify it. They tell what the subject *is*, and not what the subject *does*. Use the simple subjects which follow and add your own completers. You may add completers before the subject, after it, or both.

1. _____ Montgomery Ward _____

2. _____ ideas _____

3. _____ Liza _____

4. _____ staircases _____

5. _____ intentions _____

6. _____ camera _____

7. _____ walls _____

8. _____ silence _____

9. _____ shortness _____

10. _____ light bulbs _____

11. _____ repairs _____

12. _____ marks _____

13. _____ shoes _____

14. _____ courses _____

15. _____ Cleveland _____

16. _____ summer _____

17. _____ affection _____

18. _____ fright _____

19. _____ person _____

20. _____ knowledge _____

In each case above, you should be able to explain what meanings the completers add to the simple subject. Also, review each of your completers to be sure you still have only a subject and not a subject-plus-predicate structure. Be sure to avoid such completers as: "silence is golden." Such a case is a complete sentence rather than a complete subject.

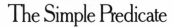

# The Simple Predicate

The basic predicate is a verb whose action is complete. Verbs give information about what a subject does, but they also give information about what a subject is. Usually we expect a verb to tell us about the action or actions of the subject, so one popular way of describing the verb is to call it an "action word." But some verbs, like "is" or "was," do not have much action in them. They are the verbs that give information about the subject's current, past, or future situation.

Our first task is to realize that not every verb can actually be a predicate in a sentence. Some verbs or verb forms need helpers or completers to have them make sense for us in a sentence. The following lists show forms of the same basic verb. The first list is a group of verbs that can serve as predicates right away. These are simple predicates. The second is a list of verb forms that cannot be predicates.

| *Simple predicate verbs* | *Verb forms that cannot be predicates* |
|---|---|
| 1. work | 1. working |
| 2. sleep | 2. to sleep |
| 3. hit | 3. hitting |
| 4. think | 4. thinking |
| 5. sharpened | 5. to sharpen |
| 6. allow | 6. allowing |
| 7. observe | 7. observing |
| 8. let | 8. letting |
| 9. see | 9. seeing |
| 10. choose | 10. to choose |

The reason that the second group of verbs cannot serve as predicates is that they do not give us a sense of completed action. This is easier to see when we put a subject with these verbs. If we are to have a sentence we must have the pattern: subject + predicate. The simplest predicate is a verb whose action is complete. The first three examples below show that pattern:

| *Subject* + | *Simple predicate* |
|---|---|
| 1. Reggie Jackson | protested |
| 2. nobody | sang |
| 3. the Central Bank | closed |

In each of these cases, all that is needed to make a sentence is capitalizing the first letter of each subject and adding a final punctuation mark—in these cases simply a period. As sentences these examples would be:

> 1. Reggie Jackson protested.
> 2. Nobody sang.
> 3. The Central Bank closed.

But if we take these verbs and use the forms that end in "-ing," or the form that begins with "to," we do not have sentences because the action is not complete. Here are the same examples with verbs that cannot be predicates:

> 1. Reggie Jackson protesting
> 2. nobody to sing
> 3. the Central Bank closing

In each of these cases the sense of having said something complete or final is missing. We keep waiting for the sentence to finish itself. The "-ing" form of the verb used above is called a participle. The "to" form of the verb is called an infinitive. Neither the participle nor the infinitive can, by itself, be a simple predicate. It is useful to learn this fact because many sentence fragments (treated below in Unit 5, "The Sentence Fragment") use the participle in place of a complete verb for the predicate.

Keep this in mind, but concentrate now on supplying simple predicates for the subjects which follow. The first five examples are done, with the simple predicate underlined. Each is a completed sentence with proper punctuation. Be sure your examples also include proper punctuation. Also, be sure that your sentences use different predicates than those we use in the samples.

1. Superman flies.

2. Edward Lewis Wallant wrote.

3. Kareem Abdul Jabbar scored.

4. The President of Guatemala resigned.

5. Rita Perez dances.

6. That idea     _____

7. The Grateful Dead     _____

8. My Uncle Toby     _____

9. No one but his aunt     _____

10. Jasper     _____

11. The woman from upstairs     _____

12. Alma with the funny hat     _____

13. Sonny Maldonado     _____

14. My friend Sammy     _____

15. Schrafft's Candy Company     _____

16. The rest of the school     _____

17. Only the Ford station wagon     _____

18. Jasper and Rita     _____

19. Against the protests of Rita, I     _____

20. Not a single one of them _____

21. After the election, Jasper _____

22. The postage stamp _____

23. Your help _____

24. The lettuce-worker's union _____

25. When she stopped laughing, Inez _____

Be sure to go over your work carefully to see that no verbs with "-ing" forms are standing alone as simple predicates. If you have some, change them to the proper form for a predicate. Or, observe the directions below and change them accordingly.

## Using the "-ing" form of the verb as a predicate

Sooner or later most of us will want to use the "-ing" form of the verb in a predicate. This can be done by adding a small completer verb, or helper verb. The helper verb is some form of the verb "to be" or "to have." The helper or completer verb when used with an "-ing" or participial form of a verb makes the action complete. Consider the following examples:

1. Reggie Jackson was protesting.
2. Nobody has been singing.
3. The Central Bank will be closing.

In each of these examples the participle has a form of the completer verb "to be"; and in the second example the verb "to be" (in the form "been") has an additional helper, "has." Some of the most common completer forms for changing the "-ing" verb to a complete verb are:

| | | | |
|---|---|---|---|
| 1. is | | 7. might be |
| 2. was | | 8. should be |
| 3. am | | 9. could be |
| 4. are | | 10. would be |
| 5. were | | 11. had been |
| 6. will be | | 12. have been |

13. might have been  17. must have been
14. should have been  18. used to be
15. could have been  19. has been
16. will have been  20. would have been

Using one of these completer forms will make any "-ing" form verb into a complete verb that can be a predicate. The first five examples below show how this can be done. In the spaces provided, convert the rest of the "-ing" form verbs into complete verbs, and therefore into predicates.

|  | *Subject* | *Predicate* |
|---|---|---|
| 1. working | Harriet | was working |
| 2. thinking | My Uncle Toby | is thinking |
| 3. hitting | Reggie Jackson | should be hitting |
| 4. sulking | Jasper | has been sulking |
| 5. dozing | Not a soul | was dozing |
| 6. shooting | Billy the Kid | _____ |
| 7. supervising | Hilda | _____ |
| 8. halting | The soldiers | _____ |
| 9. working | The tax collector | _____ |
| 10. conducting | These wires | _____ |
| 11. changing | The music | _____ |

| 12. running | All of us | _____ |
| 13. punting | The Jets | _____ |
| 14. winning | The American League | _____ |
| 15. giggling | No one with us | _____ |
| 16. calling | His Aunt Maeve | _____ |
| 17. stalling | The authorities | _____ |
| 18. whining | Freddy | _____ |
| 19. reading | Inez and Rita | _____ |
| 20. trying | The whole team | _____ |

# The Predicate with Adverb Completers

In a way, adding a helper verb to "-ing" verb forms makes a predicate with completers. But a wide variety of words can complete the simple predicate. We will concentrate on one kind of word or expression to help clarify the simple predicate. That is the kind we call adverbs—words which team up with verbs to give a more complete sense of the way the verb works.

A good general rule to help in making a predicate with an adverb completer is that adverbs usually answer questions like, When? Where? How? First we will concentrate on completers that tell when the action of the predicate verb took place or will take place.

## The predicate with completers relating to time

The first examples show the adverb completer underlined. The examples are from the last exercise.

1. Harriet was working late.
2. My Uncle Toby is thinking right now.
3. Reggie Jackson should be hitting soon.
4. Jasper had been sulking before.
5. Not a soul was dozing then.

In each of these cases the words we add complete the predicate by telling us something about the "time when" the action of the verb happens. The same thing is true of the examples below, examples which use the form of the verb which can stand alone as a simple predicate. These, too, are examples from a previous exercise.

6. Superman flies today.
7. Edward Lewis Wallant wrote long ago.
8. Kareem Abdul Jabbar scored last week.
9. The President of Guatemala resigned yesterday.
10. Rita Perez dances tonight.

Some more adverbs that tell us about time are: later, sooner, after, again, until then, tomorrow, already, instantly, often, first, always, next. There are many more than this list. In the examples below, add completers to the predicate. Be sure they tell us something about time, such as when an action occurred or will occur. Use some of the completers listed above and in the samples, but try also to use at least five new completers not included on these lists.

1. Erica writes _____ .

2. Uncle Toby was running _____ .

3. Everyone had arrived _____ .

4. My first wife scowled _____ .

5. No one could speak _____ .

6. Your girlfriend may never swim _____ .

7. We were moving  _____ .

8. Everyone spoke  _____ .

9. The Model Congress began  _____ .

10. The President of Malawi was cheered  _____ .

11. Inez was singing her song  _____ .

12. Congress voted on the bill  _____ .

13. Marta read the book  _____ .

14. Lucille will row the boat  _____ .

15. All of us will have our say  _____ .

---

**POINTER**

The last five examples above are a bit different from the first ten. Discuss the differences with your teacher or with a friend if possible. The last five examples are natural enough in the sense that most of us speak such sentences much of the time. The fact that there are words between the verb and the adverb completer should not make the sentence any harder to deal with. The point of these examples is to show that adverb completers can come later in the predicate than right after the verb.

---

### The predicate with completers relating to place

Adverb completers can tell where something happens as well as when it happens. Some typical words that can be used as completers of place are: upstairs, downstairs, underneath, there, here, next door, left, right, up, down, in, out, around, behind, in front, near, far, away, close, beyond, and beneath. There are many more than these, and in your own samples below, be sure to add at least five completers of place to this list. The five examples which follow use the same basic principles we discussed in talking about completers of time. The structure for completers of place is the same.

1. Harriet was working next door.
2. My Uncle Toby is thinking downstairs.
3. Reggie Jackson should be hitting left.
4. Jasper had been sulking there.
5. Not a soul was dozing in front.

Provide your own completers of place in the examples below. Be prepared to talk about what exact information they give readers of the sentence that they did not have before you added the completer.

1. Everyone stood _____.

2. No one was smiling _____.

3. They were running like mad _____.

4. We had some beer _____.

5. Alma Perado would not do her dance _____.

6. I wanted to be _____ Jasper.

7. Inez hid _____ her home.

8. The Air Force Captain was _____ from home.

9. We wanted someone who lived _____ New York.

10. Jasper wanted a seat _____ Rita.

---

**POINTER**

Here, too, the last five examples are a bit different from the first five. The point is that we can put completers of place in several different spots in a sentence.

---

## The predicate with completers relating to manner

Just as adverbs tell us when and where something happens, they also tell us how. The adverbs that tell us about the manner in which something happens may be the most common. There is no way of listing them all, but a short list will give some idea of how many there are and how often we use them: slowly, sharply, fast, loud, soft, dull, better, worse, stupidly, cunningly, foxily, gracefully, unhappily, miserably, excitedly, brightly, joyously, quickly, hardly, hopefully, clumsily, expertly. The list is almost endless. The first examples below are the same ones we have used before. We use these examples because it is important to realize that the same kind of verb can be completed in any of a number of ways. The way we choose depends on what we want to say or how we want to complete the sense of a predicate.

1. Harriet was working swiftly.

2. My Uncle Toby is thinking silently.

3. Reggie Jackson should be hitting better.

4. Jasper had been sulking more and more.

5. Not a soul was dozing comfortably.

Provide your own completers of manner in the examples below. Try to find as many new completers of manner as possible.

1. The Marines were landing _____ .

2. Marvin Barnes could not dribble _____ .

3. Blood Sweat and Tears played _____ .

4. The whole school protested _____ .

5. Some of us trembled _____ .

6. The idea was being rejected _____ .

7. Jasper argued _____ .

8. Inez could not scream _____ .

9. Helen Reddy spoke _____ .

10. The new ambassador whispered _____ .

The following sentences need predicate completers. You decide whether to use a completer of time, place, or manner. See, too, if you can think up any kinds of completers which do not fit into these groups. There are some others, though they are of much less importance than the ones we have described. They usually give us no trouble in everyday speech. Concentrate on making the completers you use below add clarity to the sentence. Try to write the best sentence you can. Be prepared to say whether you use a completer of time, place, or manner.

1. Luke was running _____ Janice.

2. The rhododendrons are sprouting _____

   this year.

3. I had spoken _____ .

4. The dentist _____ drilled my teeth.

5. _____

   we will go right home.

6. Rita was not seeing Jasper _____ .

7. Manolo _____ ducked the punch.

8. The subway was running _____ .

9. We all were smiling _____ .

10. _____
    everybody was shouting.

11. The people _____
    found out where Inez went.

12. Rita argued _____
    with Jasper.

13. President Jones could not decide _____ .

14. _____ the movie theater
    will show a film.

15. Nobody _____ told me.

16. The congress will act _____ .

17. The traffic commissioner could not do his job _____ .

18. We made an agreement _____ .

19. The entire class vowed it would _____
    fight.

20. Solidarity _____
    means success.

# Sentence Fragment

Probably the most common complaint many writers hear is that they do not always write complete sentences. Instead, they sometimes write fragments. A fragment is only part of a sentence. It can be a subject or a predicate each standing alone, or it can be a | subject | + | predicate | structure that is not a really completed statement, such as those structures we will treat later as subordinate clauses in Section IV.

We will concentrate first on recognition of sentence fragments. An ability to recognize fragments will help you find them in your own work. Changing them to completed sentences is just as important as identifying fragments. Both jobs are emphasized in this section.

**Fragments with no verb at all**

Sometimes a sentence fragment will appear with no verb at all. It will have a subject and possibly some of the completers which belong in the predicate, but it will have no verb to make the predicate work. A simple example follows:

| Jasper, Rita, and Inez down by the movie house with everybody else. |

In this example all we have is the subject, "Jasper, Rita, and Inez," followed by a completer of place and a completer of manner. The completer of place is "down by the movie house," and the completer of manner is "with everybody else." What we naturally ask of this example is: What are Jasper, Rita, and Inez doing? Why are they there? Is there no action? Why not? Here is one way of making this fragment into a sentence. Notice how the parts are labeled.

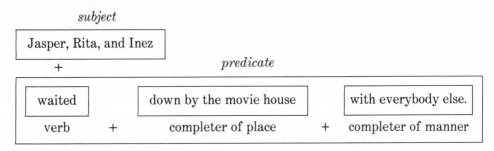

In this case, the verb "waited" makes the predicate complete. Without it, this is a fragment, not a sentence.

Another example follows. It has the same problem: no verb.

> Clyde MacDowell from a town near Peoria, Illinois.

Here, the problem is that we do not know what Clyde MacDowell did, does, or will do. All we know is that he is mentioned together with a town near Peoria. In order for this to be a complete sentence, we need a verb for the predicate. Supply a workable verb in the space provided below:

> Clyde MacDowell _____ from a town near Peoria, Illinois.

Clearly, a simple verb can make the predicate complete and turn the fragment into a sentence. In the examples below decide which ones are fragments and which are not. For each fragment, provide a verb in the space allowed, and indicate with an X just where you would place that verb in order to make the fragment a complete sentence. In sentences that are already complete, underline the subject once and the verb twice.

1. We call from home. _____

2. Nobody here but old friends. _____

3. Aunt Maeve from Evansville almost eighty-eight years old.

   _____

4. I saw fourteen robins, two cardinals, a nuthatch, and six chickadees.

   _____

5. FBI agents from Atlanta, Memphis, and Altoona. _____

6. My Uncle Toby with the long hair and the funny cigar. _____

   _____

7. Florence Nightingale near the beds of the wounded.

   _____

8. I thought of you there alone. _____

9. The photograph of three men under a large fallen tree. _____

_____

10. Four hundred thousand people with blue scarves on their heads.

_____

Go over your work, and ask your instructor to make up some more samples for you if you did not get at least half of these sentences right. Do the same for the other sections of this unit.

### Fragments with a verb that is not used as the predicate verb

It becomes more tricky to spot a fragment when it has a verb as well as a subject. The problem arises with a verb which is part of the predicate completer instead of being itself the simple predicate. The way to spot such fragments is to find the subject, then look right away for the verb which puts it into action or which gives information about it. It also helps to see exactly what the verb in the completer refers to, or, to put it differently, what its subject is. If we take the same fragment we used before and change just part of it, we can produce a fragment with a verb in it. Such fragments are hard to identify, so it is important to watch them closely.

> Jasper, Rita, and Inez down by the movie house where everybody stood around.

The situation is much as it was in the last example except that one of the completers has a verb in it: "where everybody stood around." The verb is "stood." The completer tells us "where," so it is a completer of place. For some writers, this will seem to be a sentence because it has a subject and a verb, but the problem is that the subject of the sentence is not the same subject that has the verb. Who stood around? Everybody stood around, so "everybody" is the subject of that verb. Where is the verb for "Jasper, Rita, and Inez"? It still is not there. Inserting the verb "waited" after "Inez" will turn this fragment into a sentence, just as it did before.

Other examples will show how hard these fragments are to identify. Each example below is a fragment. In each case the subject of what should be the sentence is underlined. Find the verb or verbs in the fragment, underline it, then circle its proper subject.

1. Because his mother wants him quiet, Frank in the closet.

2. Benedetto, who never liked people.

3. My friend from a place where everyone dances.

4. Wonderful Freddy under the weather if he drinks too much.

5. The suspect, whom everyone hated.

A hasty writer might let these fragments stand as sentences simply because they have a verb as well as a subject. But once one sees that the main subject of the fragment has no verb, the problem becomes clear. Below are the fragments again, but now with a proper verb which makes them into sentences. The subject is underlined once and the verb underlined twice.

1. Because his mother wants him quiet, Frank slept in the closet.

2. Benedetto, who never liked people, disappeared.

3. My friend comes from a place where everyone dances.

4. Wonderful Freddy gets under the weather if he drinks too much.

5. The suspect, whom everyone hated, died.

The following examples are either fragments or sentences. Identify each fragment and underline its subject. In the blank next to it write a verb that will make the fragment a sentence, then put an X in the place where the verb should go. In the case of complete sentences, underline the subject once and the verb twice.

1. Rita and Jasper, who stayed up late. _____

2. People near the woman who fired her shotgun. _____

3. His opinion that people never do anything by themselves. _____

4. My suspicion was that no one knew who I was. _____

5. Half the votes from those who should have known better.  _____

6. The building where my father works.  _____

7. The camera with the lens that would not focus.  _____

8. The tires when the car crashed.  _____

9. My imagination when Jasper told me all about it.  _____

10. The old songs people always wanted to hear.  _____

11. Uncle Toby when the police wanted him to testify.  _____

12. Freddy the person who never laughs.  _____

13. The newspaper for people who like to read.  _____

14. The complaints he made were never answered.  _____

15. The idea that no one ever makes the same mistakes twice.  _____

### Fragments with "-ing," "-ed," "-en" verb forms, but no predicate verb

One of the trickiest kinds of fragments to identify is the one that uses a participle in place of a verb. Participles usually end in "-ing," "-ed," or "-en." We treated this kind of verb form in Unit 3, "The Simple Predicate." Because most of the participles that give us trouble are "-ing" words, we will concentrate on them. The first example is of a fragment using the "-ing" word in place of a verb:

> Reggie Jackson hitting when we were in the kitchen.

In this fragment we get a clear idea of what the writer wished to say, but we do not get everything. We sense that the action is not yet complete. As we said in our earlier statements on "-ing" verb forms, the way to make them into real verbs is to add a helper verb. The helper is underlined in the next example, which now is a complete sentence.

> Reggie Jackson <u>was</u> hitting when we were in the kitchen.

It might help to review pages 14 and 15, where a list of helper verbs may be useful for making verbs out of "-ing" words.

Sometimes participles in the past tense, ending with "-ed," "-en," or a similar form, will give the same kind of trouble. When they are used in place of a verb they, too, need a helper verb to complete the action. An example of this is:

> My friend Inez stunned by their tone of voice.

The sense of this is not complete. The word "stunned" is only part of a verb, not the whole verb. To make the sentence complete we have to add a helper verb, such as "was" or "will be" or "had been." Such a fragment becomes a sentence when the helper is added:

> My friend Inez <u>would have been stunned</u> by their tone of voice.

The entire verb is now underlined.

Before you go on to do the exercises that follow, it will help to review the way in which participles are made into predicate verbs. Review pages 14 and 15. The problem below is to supply the helper verb needed to make the participle a predicate verb. Write the verb in the space provided and mark, with an X, the place where it should go in the sentence. A few examples below are complete sentences, but most are fragments. In the sentences that are already complete, underline the subject once and the verb twice.

1. Jasper helping out with dinner. _____

2. My ideas becoming more and more accepted by the people. _____

3. The company president filling in for Jerry Oyama. _____

4. Freddy chosen by a voice vote in the labor hall. _____

5. My invention stolen by a greedy foreman. _____

6. Alma excited by the noise of the power saw. _____

7. People stunned her with their criticism. _____

8. No one more amused by the way they sing than I. _____

9. Sam wondering which one of them was going to leave first. _____

10. If we have someone choosing first, we will be all right. _____

11. Everyone having a fine time today. _____

12. People loitering about the halls. _____

13. Fred sensing that something was up. _____

14. We having no trouble getting it together this time. _____

15. The whole family disturbed by the noise. _____

**FRAGMENT POINTER**

Go through your own writing and find at least one fragment which you thought was a sentence. Write it here:

_____

_____

_____

_____

Now rewrite the fragment as a completed sentence:

_____

_____

_____

_____

What was the problem with your fragment? How did you go about making it into a sentence? Did the fragment fall into any of the three patterns discussed here?

# The Run-on Sentence

A fragment is not enough of a structure to be a sentence, but a run-on sentence is too much of a structure for a single sentence to bear. The run-on sentence does not end when it should. It puts too much together instead of finding the best structures to express each thought. Usually what happens is that two or more sentences are joined together with no punctuation. An example follows:

> José had forty dollars he spent it all on a spree.

The simplest correction for this is to end the first sentence with a period and begin the second with a capital letter:

> José had forty dollars. He spent it all on a spree.

Another version of the problem is called the comma splice (discussed further on pages 85–87). Basically, it is the same as the examples above, except there is a comma where the end punctuation should have come in the first sentence. Such run-on sentences are tricky, because most writers feel the comma solves the problem of pausing between sentences. They do not realize that the problem arises in the first place because there are two sentences involved. An example, with its corrected version, follows:

> Marieta could not cook, after college she went to cooking school.

> Marieta could not cook. After college she went to cooking school.

The following examples all are run-on sentences. Read them carefully and correct each sentence on the lines below.

> 1. Big Lou was "chairman of the board," after lunch nobody snored as loud as he did.

2. The women played tennis under different circumstances the men played golf.

3. Everyone already saw the differences between the two of them only Martine had a chance.

4. We tried several different things, nothing worked.

5. Everyone spoke at the same time the chairman could not hear a word.

_____

_____

_____

**PUNCTUATION POINTER**
**The Semicolon**

Actually, all the examples above represent bad punctuation. One of the ways to correct the problem is to make separate sentences of the parts, as we have suggested you do. But there is another way which some writers prefer. That is to use a semicolon (;) between sentences. This has the force of a period, but it also lets the writer join two thoughts more closely together than they would be if they were separate sentences. Every one of the sentence problems above can be solved with the semicolon in this way:

The women played tennis; under different circumstances the men played golf.

Either solution is good. You may feel free to choose.

## Overloaded sentences

The problems above are created usually because the writer sees a close connection between two sentences. The failure to punctuate correctly makes the relationship unclear. Sometimes the failure is caused by accident. Sometimes it is caused by the writer's not realizing the need to relate the sentences to one another.

Many run-on sentences are not caused by problems of punctuation. They result from trying to cram too much information into one sentence. This produces the overloaded sentence. The way to fix such a sentence is to examine it carefully to see that all the subordinate clauses and phrases are clearly connected to the independent clause at the heart of the sentence. See Section IV, "Principles of Subordination," for a complete discussion of clauses and phrases. The examples below are taken from student essays. They show some typical problems shared by many writers.

---

As the story progresses all the things that Okonkwo had worked so hard for started to dissolve, at first on account of his own *chi*, or god, and later because of the coming of the white man.

---

The problem with this sentence arises at the first comma. The writer actually has a complete sentence by the time he reaches the comma, so all the remaining phrases are the overload. Technically, the phrases after the comma should be clauses. They should be attached with coordinate conjunctions (see Section III, "Coordination"). Or, they should be separated and made into a new sentence. Probably the easiest way of rewriting this sentence would be:

---

As the story progresses, all the things that Okonkwo had worked so hard for started to dissolve. At first they dissolved on account of his own *chi*, or god, and later because of the coming of the white man.

---

The elements added to the original are a comma after "progresses"; a period after "dissolve"; a capital letter for "At"; and a subject + predicate, "they dissolved," for the second sentence. The most important thing to remember about this way of solving the problem is that the overload will almost always come in the second half of the sentence. Once you realize it is an overload, you can remedy the situation by making the overload a separate sentence.

The next example is slightly different, but the solution which follows it is basically the same as that above.

---

I would have written about the friends I have met but I only know a few by name the rest by room number.

---

I would have written about the friends I have met, but I only know a few by name. The rest I know by room number.

---

The following examples are all drawn from actual essays. Study them carefully and rewrite them in order to avoid the run-on sentence. If the sentence is poorly punctuated, offer a new punctuation. If the sentence is overloaded, make the overload into a separate sentence. If both problems exist, offer both solutions.

---

1. In a society where a man's status is judged by his strength and bravery, and how a man takes care of his household Unoka would not do his harvesting until the last moment he was too busy drinking palm wine and playing the flute.

---

_____

_____

_____

_____

_____

_____

---

2. Fred appears in another situation where he is seen in a market, there a customer takes for granted that he is one of the employees.

---

_____

_____

_____

_____

3. Fred was accused of a crime that he did not commit because Fred happened to be black and around at the time, he was picked up by the police, beaten and forced to sign a confession which he was not allowed to read.

_____

_____

_____

_____

_____

4. He felt that he would not be noticeable to people, because he had stayed in that cave and he had forgotten about people this was while he thought the man did not see him.

_____

_____

_____

_____

_____

5.  After a dream has been put off it does not just shrink up and fade away, it isn't thought of and then rubbed out like a sore, it has no odor of anything rotten, but it doesn't have sweetness either, it's just there.

_____

_____

_____

_____

_____

_____

_____

6.  He keeps moving off a little further and further and the pitcher throws the ball and he is off it is all up to him now no one else.

_____

_____

_____

_____

_____

_____

---

> 7. By having this crash, Todd found himself, this is where the story's title "Flying Home" comes in.

---

_____

_____

_____

_____

Correcting someone else's writing can be very helpful, but it is probably even more helpful to correct your own work. Go through some of your recent writing and find examples of run-on or overloaded sentences. Write each one in the first space provided, then write your revision of the sentence. Be prepared to talk about the ways in which you made your revision.

**Your run-on sentence:** _____

_____

_____

_____

**Your revision:** _____

_____

_____

_____

**Your run-on sentence:** _____

_____

_____

_____

**Your revision:** _____

_____

_____

_____

**Your run-on sentence:** _____

_____

_____

**Your revision:** _____

# Subject and Predicate Agreement

One basic problem many writers share is making the subject agree with the predicate. If the subject talks about a number of things, then the predicate must have a plural verb. If the subject talks about only one thing, then the predicate needs a singular verb. We can visualize it by referring to the following diagram:

| | | |
|---|---|---|
| singular subject | + | singular predicate verb |
| plural subject | + | plural predicate verb |

Either one of those patterns is correct, but any time that a singular subject is followed by a plural verb in the predicate we have trouble. This is what we wish to avoid. The reasons such problems exist for writers are many. One reason is forgetting to check for agreement, particularly after you have changed your mind about whether to use a singular or plural subject. Another is not being able to identify singular subjects and plural subjects or singular verbs and plural verbs. A third reason is that in some long sentences it is easy to lose track of the verb when it is far away from its subject.

## Identifying singular and plural subjects

The most common rule for making a subject plural is to add an "-s" or "-es" to the end of the subject. Some examples of the way we can make a singular subject plural are listed below.

| Singular subject | Subject made plural |
|---|---|
| 1. boat | 1. boats |
| 2. basketball game | 2. basketball games |
| 3. city | 3. cities |
| 4. terrorist | 4. terrorists |
| 5. rumor | 5. rumors |
| 6. newspaper | 6. newspapers |
| 7. neighborhood | 7. neighborhoods |
| 8. soap opera | 8. soap operas |
| 9. spy | 9. spies |
| 10. radio | 10. radios |

Trouble with forming "-s" plurals often comes from not pronouncing the "-s" in everyday speech. Visual double-checking can help in such situations. But there are some words which do not follow the "-s" or "-es" rule. They have their own rules, and we must learn them simply by seeing them and remembering them. Some of the most important follow.

| Singular subject | Subject made plural |
|---|---|
| 1. woman | 1. women |
| 2. deer | 2. deer |
| 3. datum | 3. data |
| 4. criterion | 4. criteria |
| 5. child | 5. children |
| 6. mouse | 6. mice |
| 7. foot | 7. feet |
| 8. tooth | 8. teeth |
| 9. crisis | 9. crises |
| 10. phenomenon | 10. phenomena |

Then there is another group of problem words which give some of us trouble because they sound plural but are really singular. Some of them are: box, silence, voice, vice, nonsense, importance, climax, diligence. Just because a word sounds as if it ends with an "-s," do not assume it is plural. Check it carefully by looking at it.

A few words also have a plural ending though they are singular in meaning. These are tough ones and must be learned separately. Some of the most useful and important ones are: politics, economics, mathematics, measles, physics.

In the following list, decide whether the form of the subject given is singular or plural. Put a check mark in the correct box to indicate which choice you make. Then, in the space provided, write in either the missing plural or the singular form of the subject. In other words, if the form shown is singular, your job is to write the plural form. If the form shown is plural, write the singular.

| Subject | Singular | Plural | Supply the other form |
|---|---|---|---|
| 1. distance | ☐ | ☐ | _____ |
| 2. beginnings | ☐ | ☐ | _____ |
| 3. solution | ☐ | ☐ | _____ |
| 4. density | ☐ | ☐ | _____ |
| 5. Englishman | ☐ | ☐ | _____ |
| 6. touchdown | ☐ | ☐ | _____ |
| 7. instances | ☐ | ☐ | _____ |
| 8. corpse | ☐ | ☐ | _____ |
| 9. recollections | ☐ | ☐ | _____ |
| 10. person | ☐ | ☐ | _____ |
| 11. sheep | ☐ | ☐ | _____ |
| 12. avenue | ☐ | ☐ | _____ |
| 13. Japanese | ☐ | ☐ | _____ |

| Subject | Singular | Plural | Supply the other form |
|---------|----------|--------|-----------------------|
| 14. country | ☐ | ☐ | _____ |
| 15. knives | ☐ | ☐ | _____ |

## Singular and plural predicates

The problem with making the predicate agree with its subject usually arises only in the third-person singular and plural. The rule for making the third-person verb singular is opposite that for making a subject singular. Adding "-s" to the third-person plural verb usually makes the verb singular. Taking the "-s" away makes it plural. In the following list the verb has a third-person subject along with it to make the pattern clear.

| Third-person singular verb | Third-person plural verb |
|---------------------------|--------------------------|
| 1. Geoffrey helps | 1. they help |
| 2. he thinks | 2. they think |
| 3. she does | 3. the girls do |
| 4. it is | 4. people are |
| 5. one strikes | 5. all strike |
| 6. everyone has | 6. the officers have |
| 7. no one sees | 7. they see |
| 8. everybody satisfies | 8. individuals satisfy |
| 9. the law allows | 9. parents allow |
| 10. nothing suggests | 10. instructors suggest |

Most of the trouble with singular verbs comes in the present tense. In the past tense we usually use the same verb form for singular and for plural. The past-tense forms of the verbs listed above are singular *and* plural depending on the subject you link them with: helped, thought, did, struck, had, saw, satisfied, allowed, suggested. The only verb left out of the list above is number four, "is/are." Like some of the subjects, it follows its own rules. The past singular form is "was"; the past plural form is "were." We simply have to commit that one to memory. The conjugation of the verb "to be" follows:

| Present tense | Past tense |
|---------------|------------|
| I am | I was |
| you are | you were |
| he, she, it is | he, she, it was |
| we are | we were |
| you are | you were |
| they are | they were |

In the following list decide whether the form of the verb supplied is singular or plural and indicate what you think it is in the box next to it. Then supply either the third-person singular or the plural form of the verb, depending on which one is not presently there. If we have supplied the singular form, you supply the plural form.

| *Third-person verb* | *Singular* | *Plural* | *Supply the other form* |
|---|---|---|---|
| 1. presents | ☐ | ☐ | _____ |
| 2. were | ☐ | ☐ | _____ |
| 3. knock | ☐ | ☐ | _____ |
| 4. preach | ☐ | ☐ | _____ |
| 5. stops | ☐ | ☐ | _____ |
| 6. harm | ☐ | ☐ | _____ |
| 7. intensify | ☐ | ☐ | _____ |
| 8. mean | ☐ | ☐ | _____ |
| 9. tries | ☐ | ☐ | _____ |
| 10. build | ☐ | ☐ | _____ |
| 11. eliminate | ☐ | ☐ | _____ |
| 12. strive | ☐ | ☐ | _____ |
| 13. turns | ☐ | ☐ | _____ |

| *Third-person verb* | *Singular* | *Plural* | *Supply the other form* |
|---|---|---|---|
| 14. know | ☐ | ☐ | _____ |
| 15. accents | ☐ | ☐ | _____ |

## Making the subject and predicate agree

Now, the most important point to remember is that the subject and predicate must always be either both singular or both plural. The samples which follow below are in agreement. Next to them, indicate whether the subjects and predicates are singular or plural.

|  | *Singular* | *Plural* |
|---|---|---|
| 1. Jasper never quits. | ☐ | ☐ |
| 2. Either Rita or Tony is wacky. | ☐ | ☐ |
| 3. Each of the movies we saw was crummy. | ☐ | ☐ |
| 4. Reggie Jackson hit four homers. | ☐ | ☐ |
| 5. Uncle Toby and Aunt Belle cried all the way home. | ☐ | ☐ |
| 6. Nobody wants a fight. | ☐ | ☐ |
| 7. We will not leave here. | ☐ | ☐ |
| 8. Everyone was waiting at home. | ☐ | ☐ |
| 9. The women wanted quiet. | ☐ | ☐ |
| 10. People don't know what they want. | ☐ | ☐ |

In the first five examples below, supply the proper form of either the subject or predicate, and check whether it is singular or plural. Choose a subject or a predicate which will make good sense. Then go on in the next ten examples to choose both your own subject and your own predicate, being sure to keep them in agreement. If it is a singular subject, then the predicate must be singular. If it is a plural subject, then the predicate must be a plural.

|  | *Singular* | *Plural* |
|---|---|---|
| 1. _____ wants to go home. | ☐ | ☐ |
| 2. Aunt May and her friend _____. | ☐ | ☐ |

|  |  | Singular | Plural |
|---|---|:---:|:---:|
| 3. Each investigator _____. | | ☐ | ☐ |
| 4. _____ care about us. | | ☐ | ☐ |
| 5. Your cousin Janice _____. | | ☐ | ☐ |
| 6. _____. | | ☐ | ☐ |
| 7. _____. | | ☐ | ☐ |
| 8. _____. | | ☐ | ☐ |
| 9. _____. | | ☐ | ☐ |
| 10. _____. | | ☐ | ☐ |
| 11. _____. | | ☐ | ☐ |
| 12. _____. | | ☐ | ☐ |
| 13. _____. | | ☐ | ☐ |
| 14. _____. | | ☐ | ☐ |
| 15. _____. | | ☐ | ☐ |

# 8

# Pronoun Agreement

A special problem which often makes sentences unclear is that of faulty pronoun agreement. Simply put, this means the matching of a pronoun with the noun it refers to elsewhere in the sentence. It also means the matching of a singular or plural pronoun with its singular or plural verb. Because subordinate clauses sometimes come between a pronoun and its verb, unusual difficulties can arise. The principles discussed earlier concerning subject and verb agreement are relevant here. If the pronoun is singular, its verb must be singular. If the noun referred to is singular, the pronoun which refers to it must also be singular.

The following list offers some of the most common pronouns which are likely to give you trouble.

| *Pronouns* | | |
|---|---|---|
| 1. which | 6. its | 11. themselves |
| 2. that | 7. each | 12. nobody |
| 3. one | 8. their | 13. _____ |
| 4. who | 9. someone | 14. _____ |
| 5. anyone | 10. everybody | 15. _____ |

The empty spaces are for you to add your own examples, since there may be some special problems you will want to take note of for future reference.

The following examples offer the pronoun in proper agreement both with its noun referent and with its verb. In each case the word the pronoun refers to is underlined and labeled "ref."; the pronoun is labeled; and the verb is marked "verb sing." or "verb pl."

1. Joan was nobody to fool around with.
   ref. | verb sing. | pronoun

2. Pollution is a problem that has immediate priority.
   ref. | pronoun | verb sing.

3. Each of the men has his own car.
   ref. | verb sing. | pronoun

4. This   is   something   which   we must take up later.
         ‾verb‾   ‾ref.‾   pronoun
         sing.

5. She is a   woman   who   has stood   her   ground for years.
            ‾ref.‾   pronoun   ‾verb‾   pronoun
                              sing.

6. Most   of the choristers   sing   their   own song.
   ‾ref.‾                    ‾verb pl.‾ pronoun

7. The   carful   of party-goers   lost   its   way.
         ‾ref.‾                    ‾verb‾  pronoun
                                   sing.

8. I went to   California,   which   has   a vital tourist trade.
              ‾ref.‾   pronoun   ‾verb‾
                                 sing.

9. Movie stars   think   of   themselves   as something special.
   ‾ref.‾   ‾verb pl.‾      pronoun

10. Today the   lawmakers   are   all   in agreement.
              ‾ref.‾   ‾verb pl.‾ pronoun

11. The   citizens   have   a right to   their   opinions.
          ‾ref.‾   ‾verb pl.‾          pronoun

12. These are   people   who   are   unhappy with the situation.
              ‾ref.‾   pronoun   ‾verb pl.‾

These sentences do not represent every problem of agreement one is likely to encounter in writing. But the problems here are potentially serious. A writer must keep in mind the fact that pronouns must refer to a noun, and must be in agreement with that noun. It is also important to keep in mind that the pronoun must be in agreement with its verb or with the verb of the word it refers to. Perhaps you will have noticed that some of the sentences above have some pronouns which are not underlined. Sentence 12, for instance, has the pronoun "These" beginning it. "I" begins sentence 8. "She" begins sentence 5. These words are not underlined because the problems one is likely to encounter relate to other pronouns in the sentence. However, it is very important to keep in mind that pronouns can be troublesome at any time and should be watched carefully.

In the following examples, choose a pronoun which will work in the context of the sentence. You may choose a pronoun from the list on page 47 or another pronoun. In the first few sentences the word the pronoun refers to is underlined and marked "ref." In the next sentences, supply the underlining for the word the pronoun refers to.

1. Nancy and Edgar have _____ own way of doing
   *ref.*
   things.

2. Each of the diplomats took _____ place in the
   *ref.*
   conference.

3. People do not want _____ freedoms limited.
   *ref.*

4. Each problem has _____ own solution.
   *ref.*

5. Not all car owners have an uncle _____ can fix

   mufflers.

6. They are a family who love _____ peace and quiet.

7. We are _____ in this together.

8. The computers in the nation's space museum have _____

   own names.

9. Each of the football players has _____ own locker.

10. None of the companies wants _____ name mentioned.

11. Many thieves consider _____ justified in stealing.

12. Not every society has _____ survival at stake.

Problems with pronoun agreement are very persistent. You may find that even if you do these exercises correctly, the problems will show up in your writing. For this reason it is important to go through your own writing, both now and later, for examples of faulty pronoun agreement. Your teacher probably will have marked some instances of this in your work. Where this is so, write the faulty sentence and then correct it. If it turns out you have no examples of faulty agreement to choose from, write a few examples of sentences which use pronouns in proper agreement.

**Your original sentence:** _____

_____

_____

_____

**Your sentence corrected:** _____

_____

_____

_____

**Your original sentence:** _____

_____

_____

_____

**Your sentence corrected:** _____

_____

_____

_____

_____

_____

# constructing clauses and phrases

# 1

# The Independent Clause

The independent clause is the only kind of $\boxed{\text{subject}}$ + $\boxed{\text{predicate}}$ structure that can be a sentence. A sentence like

| subject | + | predicate |
|---|---|---|
| Jimmy Manolo | | worshipped his father. |

is both a sentence *and* an independent clause. One reason for having two names for a $\boxed{\text{subject}}$ + $\boxed{\text{predicate}}$ structure such as this one is that some sentences are made of two or more independent clauses. When that is true we need names for each part so we can tell what we are doing. What we must know is that no sentence is complete unless it has at least one independent clause.

The independent clause always has a subject and a predicate and makes a complete statement. It can stand alone as a sentence. Sometimes an independent clause has completers added to it, but it does not *need* them. One can develop a good sense of what an independent clause is and what it looks like by studying the examples which follow. The work done in Section I of this book should help in identifying independent clauses. Work on subject-predicate agreement and on sentence fragments should be kept in mind when studying the independent clause.

All the examples following are independent clauses. They all have their subject and predicate boxed and identified. Read them aloud to reinforce the way independent clauses sound. S is for subject, P for predicate.

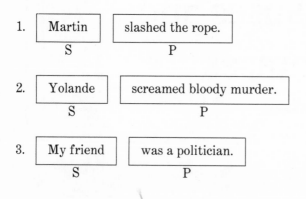

1. $\boxed{\text{Martin}}$ $\boxed{\text{slashed the rope.}}$
   $\quad$ S $\qquad\quad$ P

2. $\boxed{\text{Yolande}}$ $\boxed{\text{screamed bloody murder.}}$
   $\quad$ S $\qquad\qquad$ P

3. $\boxed{\text{My friend}}$ $\boxed{\text{was a politician.}}$
   $\quad$ S $\qquad\quad$ P

4. | The idea | | hit him suddenly. |
   S          P

5. | Sam | | settled himself on the barge. |
   S          P

6. | Aretha | | brought it all home. |
   S          P

7. | No one | | had the nerve of a guy like Jimmy. |
   S          P

8. | Your old Uncle Toby | | was a hit. |
   S          P

9. | We all | | wanted Rita back home. |
   S          P

10. | Joshua | | fought the battle of Jericho. |
    S          P

11. | The President | | argued with Congress. |
    S          P

12. | The Supremes | | have twenty million-copy records. |
    S          P

13. | The newly formed republic of Malawi | | is politically stable. |
    S          P

14. | Our old stage | | is too small. |
    S          P

15. | Fright | | makes cowards of us all. |
    S          P

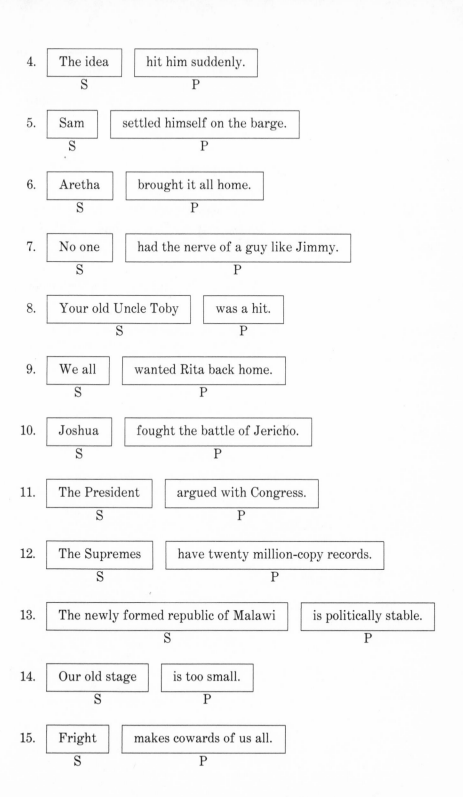

All these examples are very similar to the examples of complete sentences you have seen in earlier exercises. What they lack, when they lack anything, is extra completers to add information or to clarify points.

The following list has some independent clauses and some structures which are not independent clauses. Circle the number of each example that is an independent clause. Use these questions to decide if the structure is an independent clause:

1. Does it have both a subject and a predicate?
2. Can it stand by itself as a sentence?

Be sure to box the subject and the predicate. Put an "S" under the subject and a "P" under the predicate for identification. If the example is not an independent clause, but has either a subject or predicate, box it and identify it.

1. Only our very best friend Margarita and her bashful cousins from Peru.

2. Sleep is good for you.

3. Doin' it.

4. Before writing home for money.

5. Stop-and-go traffic knocks hell out of tires.

6. Beginning to see the light.

7. We don't know them at all.

8. CBS News covers political developments.

9. After having covered all the possibilities.

10. We caused trouble.

11. Your idea was really for the birds.

12. Ralph Ellison writing the great American novel.

13. The people will not stand for more of this.

14. Jasper was falling off his tricycle.

15. Joy, joy, joy.

16. Labor unions can't fool around now.

17. Working in the fields all day.

18. I had no friends as a kid.

19. That is all right with me.

20. This weariness and this agony in waiting.

Spaces are provided below for you to write your own independent clauses. Follow the pattern of [ subject ] + [ predicate ] and box each of them with an "S" or a "P" under them for identification. A quick review of what you did in Section I of this book will help you if you had trouble with the twenty examples above. Be sure to review those examples carefully if you have discussed them or if they have been corrected.

1. _____

2. _____

3. _____

4. _____

5. _____

6. _____

7. _____

8. _____

9. _____

10. _____

11. _____

12. _____

13. _____

14. _____

15. _____

16. _____

17. _____

18. _____

19. _____

20. _____

# The Subordinate Clause

Some ⎡ subject ⎤ + ⎡ predicate ⎤ structures are independent clauses. Some are not. Every clause must have a ⎡ subject ⎤ + ⎡ predicate ⎤ or else it is not a clause at all. All non-independent clauses are called subordinate. You may know the name "dependent" for these clauses. They are the same.

We call them subordinate because they are clauses that give information about the where, why, how, what for, and when of the independent clause. They give information, offer descriptions, and supply details which can make the independent clause much more exact in meaning. We can think of subordinate clauses as completers which have a ⎡ subject ⎤ + ⎡ predicate ⎤

The structure of most subordinate clauses is a bit different from the clauses we have already discussed. Usually a special word or group of words begins the subordinate clause. Some of them are the very same words we described in Section I, Unit 4, "The Predicate with Adverb Completers." The adverbs of time, place, and manner often introduce a subordinate clause. Because these words come ahead of the subject, they make it hard to see the ⎡ subject ⎤ + ⎡ predicate ⎤ pattern. In our work with the subordinate clause, we will call these beginning words *subordinators*. Subordinators tell us pretty quickly that the clause following is subordinate.

The examples below have the subordinator clearly labeled, and the subject and predicate of the clause itself are both labeled for clarity.

⎡ before ⎤      ⎡ we ⎤      ⎡ go home ⎤

subordinator   +   subject   +   predicate

The clause, "before we go home," needs something to complete it. Because it leads us to expect that the writer will tell us what happened or needs to happen before we go home, the clause is subordinate. It needs more clarification. The same pattern is followed in each of the following examples. Each subordinator, subject, and predicate is identified.

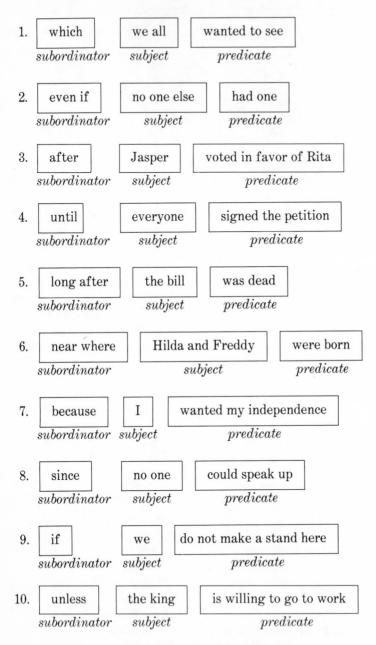

1. | which | we all | wanted to see |
   subordinator | subject | predicate

2. | even if | no one else | had one |
   subordinator | subject | predicate

3. | after | Jasper | voted in favor of Rita |
   subordinator | subject | predicate

4. | until | everyone | signed the petition |
   subordinator | subject | predicate

5. | long after | the bill | was dead |
   subordinator | subject | predicate

6. | near where | Hilda and Freddy | were born |
   subordinator | subject | predicate

7. | because | I | wanted my independence |
   subordinator | subject | predicate

8. | since | no one | could speak up |
   subordinator | subject | predicate

9. | if | we | do not make a stand here |
   subordinator | subject | predicate

10. | unless | the king | is willing to go to work |
    subordinator | subject | predicate

In each of these examples, the clause needs another statement to make full sense. For instance, we ask about example 9, "if we do not make a stand here," just what will happen? The subordinator "if" sets up expectations, and the clause that follows does not answer those expectations. We can answer those expectations ourselves by providing an independent clause in this manner:

| If we do not make a stand here, | | we will be wiped out. |
|---|---|---|
| subordinate clause | + | independent clause |

Now we have a sentence, because a complete statement has been made in the independent clause.

---

**PUNCTUATION POINTER**

In the examples which follow and in the example directly above, a comma comes after the subordinate clause that begins a sentence. Be sure to remember this pointer, since it helps clarify the relationship of a subordinate clause to a main clause. If an independent clause begins the sentence, usually no comma is necessary.

---

In the following examples, box and identify the subordinator, the subject, and the predicate of each subordinate clause. If the clause is independent, capitalize the first letter and put a period at the end of the sentence. If the example is not a clause at all, write whether it needs a subject or a predicate to make it complete.

1. no one but our own Althea

2. if afterwards we get our independence

3. by not wanting the car

4. unless everyone goes along with us

5. when we are good and ready

6. now we do not want any trouble

7. while I am getting your things

8. before Jasper has to say it again

9. after I have a good talk with my lawyer

10. up until now

11. way back when Reggie was a minor leaguer

12. whenever he sat himself down

13. however you want to do it

14. depending on what really happens

15. as we go along

16. when all the shouting dies down

17. where we used to go for dinner

18. up to their old tricks again

19. after my lollipop fell on the tile floor

20. until the people do what they really want


In the spaces supplied below, write your own subordinate clauses. In the first three examples, separate lines are provided for subordinator, subject, and predicate. The rest have simply one line, so that you can have more "elbow room." Be sure that all your subordinate clauses have subordinators first and that they also have both a subject and a predicate.

|            | *Subordinator* | *Subject* | *Predicate* |
|------------|----------------|-----------|-------------|
| 1.         | _____  | _____ | _____ |
| 2.         | _____  | _____ | _____ |
| 3.         | _____  | _____ | _____ |
| 4.         | _____ | | |
| 5.         | _____ | | |
| 6.         | _____ | | |
| 7.         | _____ | | |
| 8.         | _____ | | |
| 9.         | _____ | | |
| 10.        | _____ | | |
| 11.        | _____ | | |
| 12.        | _____ | | |
| 13.        | _____ | | |
| 14.        | _____ | | |
| 15.        | _____ | | |

One way to make a sentence using one of the subordinate clauses above is to follow this pattern:

| Subordinate clause | + | , | + | independent clause. |

The first letter should be capitalized. A comma follows the subordinate clause, and a period ends the sentence. In the spaces below take any five of the subordinate clauses in the examples above and write them on the subordinate-clause line that follows. Then add your own independent clause to complete the sense of the subordinate clause and make a sentence. An example follows:

1. Sub. clause   After Jasper voted in favor of Rita,

   Ind. clause   we knew her election was certain.

2. Sub. clause   _____

   Ind. clause   _____

3. Sub. clause   _____

   Ind. clause   _____

4. Sub. clause   _____

   Ind. clause   _____

5. Sub. clause   _____

   Ind. clause   _____

6. Sub. clause   _____

   Ind. clause   _____

7. Sub. clause   _____

   Ind. clause   _____

8. Sub. clause   _____

   Ind. clause   _____

9. Sub. clause   _____

   Ind. clause   _____

10. Sub. clause   _____

   Ind. clause   _____

# The Participial Phrase

Every | subject | + | predicate | structure is a clause. If either the subject or the predicate is missing, we have a phrase. The phrase can have either the subject or the predicate in it, but never both. Three kinds of phrases will be emphasized here: the participial phrase in this exercise, the prepositional phrase, and the infinitive phrase. The following group offers five examples of the participial phrase.

> Waving her hands in the air
> Trying to promote peace in the world
> Having begun the story
> Unveiling the monument
> Wanting a general amnesty

In each of these the subject is missing. We do not know who waves her hands, who tries to promote peace, or who began the story. It is not quite right to call these predicates, either, since there is only an "-ing" form of the verb without a helper in each one. For them to be true predicates, the "-ing" verb forms—which are called participles—need a helper verb. See page 14 in Section I, Unit 3, "The Simple Predicate," for review of helper verbs with participles. Since a useful list of participles appears there, it would be good to review pages 11–16 now.

The following participial phrases have the participle underlined:

1. <u>Following</u> the parade
2. <u>Beginning</u> the work over again
3. <u>Striking</u> a blow for freedom
4. <u>Having</u> the time of her life
5. <u>Enjoying</u> the sunshine and fresh air

The first letter of each example is capitalized because participial phrases often begin sentences. In each of these cases, the subject of the participial phrase is not mentioned and must be mentioned soon when the phrase is combined with an independent clause to make a sentence. Every one of these participial phrases can be made into a sentence by following this pattern:

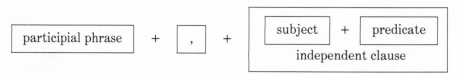

**PARTICIPIAL POINTER**
The participial phrase has its subject right after the comma which follows every participial phrase starting a sentence. The *dangling participial* phrase has no subject right after it. The reason the phrase dangles is that there is no way to know who or what is doing the action the phrase talks about. In any of the examples above, the subject of the participle must come immediately after the phrase. If another subject—that of a subordinate clause, for instance—comes

right away, the whole sense of the participial phrase is lost. The right way to do it is this way:

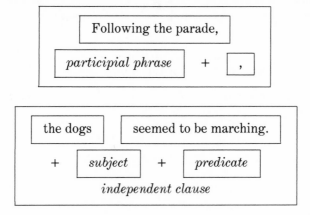

The clever thing here is that the subject, "the dogs," is served by two structures: the participial phrase and the predicate.

Study the examples of participial phrases that follow. Note that each needs a subject to help complete its sense. Then, on the lines that follow, write some participial phrases of your own. Immediately after each one, write in a suitable subject. Study the examples first.

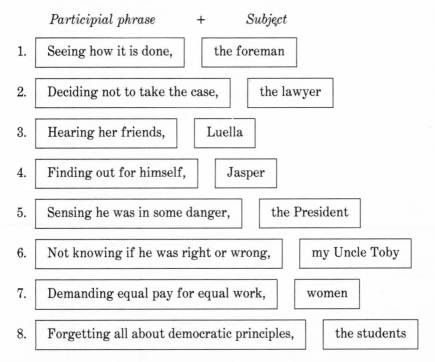

*Participial phrase*     +     *Subject*

1. Seeing how it is done,     the foreman

2. Deciding not to take the case,     the lawyer

3. Hearing her friends,     Luella

4. Finding out for himself,     Jasper

5. Sensing he was in some danger,     the President

6. Not knowing if he was right or wrong,     my Uncle Toby

7. Demanding equal pay for equal work,     women

8. Forgetting all about democratic principles,     the students

9. | Wanting nothing more than a little nap, | I

10. | Leaving everyone else behind, | the company

You may wish to consult a list of participles on pages 11 and 69 before doing this assignment. Don't forget the comma after the phrase.

*Participial phrase* + *Subject*

1. _____     _____

2. _____     _____

3. _____     _____

4. _____     _____

5. _____     _____

6. _____     _____

7. _____     _____

8. _____     _____

9. _____     _____

10. _____     _____

## Participial phrases: past tense and present perfect tense

The "-ing" participles are in the present tense. But phrases can also start with participles in the past tense or the present perfect tense, using "have" as a helper verb. If we take the ten examples of participial phrases we just used, the present tense, past tense, and present perfect tense forms look like this:

| Present tense | Past tense | Present perfect tense |
|---|---|---|
| 1. seeing | seen | having seen |
| 2. deciding | decided | having decided |
| 3. hearing | heard | having heard |
| 4. finding | found | having found |
| 5. sensing | sensed | having sensed |
| 6. knowing | known | having known |
| 7. demanding | demanded | having demanded |
| 8. forgetting | forgotten | having forgotten |
| 9. wanting | wanted | having wanted |
| 10. leaving | left | having left |

We can make participial phrases out of these past and present perfect forms just as easily as we can out of the "-ing" forms. Again, the subject of the phrase must always follow the comma which follows the phrase. If it does not, the phrase is a dangling participial phrase. Here are examples of phrases built with the past tense and present perfect tense participles listed above. A subject follows the comma.

1. Having seen the job, the foreman
2. Having decided against the case, the lawyer
3. Heard by her friends, Luella
4. Having found Rita, Jasper
5. Sensed by the President, the would-be assassin
6. Known as a fair man, my Uncle Toby
7. Having made demands, the women's organization
8. Having forgotten its democratic principles, the country
9. Wanted for third-degree assault, I
10. Having left everyone else, the company

Below, try to take the same participles you used on page 68. Put them into the past or present perfect tense and rewrite the phrase in order to make good sense.

*Participial phrase* + *Subject*

1. _____   _____

2. _____   _____

3. _____   _____

4. _____   _____

5. _____    _____

6. _____    _____

7. _____    _____

8. _____    _____

9. _____    _____

10. _____    _____

# The Prepositional Phrase

Like the last phrase discussed, the prepositional phrase begins with the word
that gives it its name: the preposition. But unlike the participial phrase, the
prepositional phrase does not usually come only at the start of a sentence.
Usually, it appears deep within the sentence. It can be part of a completer in
a predicate or in the subject. You have already seen and written many
prepositional phrases, so your two objectives here will be to identify them for
future use and to learn how to use them effectively.

We begin with a few examples of prepositional phrases. The preposition
is underlined.

1. <u>with</u> my Uncle Toby
2. <u>at</u> Anna's reunion
3. <u>from</u> the Soviet Union
4. <u>to</u> the Brooklyn Bridge
5. <u>by</u> the president himself

6. for Hilda's cold
7. with no one's help
8. in time
9. within the allotted space
10. of my own needs

The structure of a prepositional phrase can be described as
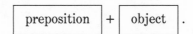 preposition + name of something. There is no predicate verb in the
prepositional phrase. At the same time we can't call the second part of the
prepositional phrase a subject. Just as the "-ing" verb form is related to the
predicate verb but is not one, the second part of the prepositional phrase is
related to the subject but is not one. We call it the object of the preposition,
but it is still the name of something. Therefore, it is more exact to describe
the structure of the prepositional phrase in this way:

preposition + object .

Using the prepositions in the examples above, write ten prepositional
phrases of your own.

1. _____

2. _____

3. _____

4. _____

5. _____

6. _____

7. _____

8. _____

9. _____

10. _____


Have your work above checked carefully. If it is satisfactory, continue. If not, review the introductory material and study the Prepositional-Phrase Pointer that follows.

---

### PREPOSITIONAL-PHRASE POINTER
The first part of a prepositional phrase raises a question. The second part answers it. When we begin a phrase with a preposition such as "to," we are setting up expectations. We naturally ask, "to" what? or, "to" whom? The answer in our example 4 above is the second part of the phrase, "the Brooklyn Bridge." The preposition asks a question and its object answers it.

---

### Special prepositions

The prepositions used in the first examples are simple prepositions, the most common in our language. But there is a very important group of prepositions which are closely related to adverbs. These prepositions are different from the adverbs discussed in Section I, Unit 4, "Predicate with Adverb Completers." Taking a moment to compare those with the list of adverb-prepositions which follows will help you see the difference.

The prepositions that follow can answer questions related to time, place, manner, and reason why. In this sense they are very much like adverbs. The phrases we build with such prepositions act as adverb completers. In this sense they are very useful in any sentence. Some of the more common prepositions that can act as adverb completers are:

*Related to time*:   after, before, since, until, up to
*Related to place*:   near, by, in, out of, through, toward, at
*Related to manner and reason why*:   with, without, in, by, because of, on account of

Here are several of these prepositions with objects. Two examples are given for each of the prepositional uses above. You can see how these prepositional phrases resemble adverbs.

*Time*:     1. after him
            2. until Christmas
*Place*:    1. near Santa Cruz
            2. by my side

*Manner*    1. with an odd look
   *and*
*reason*    2. because of rain
*why*:

---

**POINTER**

In order to be sure the prepositional phrase is really a prepositional phrase, put the preposition immediately before its object. Otherwise, you might actually write a subordinate clause. This is discussed in Section IV, "Principles of Subordination." In these exercises, then, be sure that you are writing a phrase. Do not bring in any verbs.

---

In the spaces below write some prepositional phrases that can be used as adverb completers. Use some of the prepositions mentioned above and some others if you wish.

1. _____

2. _____

3. _____

4. _____

5. _____

6. _____

7. _____

8. _____

9. _____

10. _____

# 5

# The Infinitive Phrase

When the simple predicate was discussed in Section I, Unit 3, the question of verb forms that were not predicate verbs came up. We talked about "-ing" verb forms and said that they could become predicate verbs only with a helper. There is another verb form that cannot serve as a predicate verb. This is called the infinitive:

| | | |
|---|---|---|
| 1. to go | 8. to give | 15. to arrest |
| 2. to be | 9. to receive | 16. to argue |
| 3. to have | 10. to show | 17. to kiss |
| 4. to decide | 11. to imagine | 18. to simplify |
| 5. to change | 12. to organize | 19. to barrage |
| 6. to run | 13. to agree | 20. to scream |
| 7. to begin | 14. to protest | |

There is a simple way to use such verb forms in a sentence. We make them into infinitive phrases. The structure of the infinitive phrase is described as: | infinitive | + | completer | . What we said about the prepositional phrase works here, too. The infinitive sets up a question and the completer answers it. Take the examples above. We ask of 1, "to go" where? We ask of 2, "to be" what? We can ask similar questions of all the infinitives above. The only way to get an answer is to supply a completer. Ten infinitive phrases follow:

1. to go all the way home
2. to be a playwright
3. to have enough time
4. to decide nothing
5. to change the world
6. to run the office
7. to begin the meeting
8. to give a present
9. to receive two presents
10. to show your pass

When you write your own infinitive phrases below, you may use the infinitives listed above from number 11 to 20, or you may choose completely different ones. Remember to follow the infinitive with its completer. The completer ought to be the name of something.

1. _____

2. _____

3. _____

4. _____

5. _____

6. _____

7. _____

8. _____

9. _____

10. _____

## Using the infinitive phrase in a sentence

The most basic way to use the infinitive phrase is as a subject in a clause. The predicate can be very much like any other predicate, but the subject is the entire infinitive phrase. The pattern is:

$$\boxed{\text{infinitive phrase}} \quad + \quad \boxed{\text{predicate}}$$

This pattern produces an independent clause, which when standing alone is a sentence. Several examples follow. The infinitive phrase is boxed and labeled as the subject. The predicate is boxed and labeled as the predicate.

| 1. | To run the office | was his most serious ambition. |
| | *subject* | *predicate* |

| 2. | To have a million dollars | would probably make him happy. |
| | *subject* | *predicate* |

| 3. | To see the Eiffel Tower | will be a great thrill. |
| | *subject* | *predicate* |

| 4. | To be an influential person | is the desire of Rita's sister. |
| | *subject* | *predicate* |

| 5. | To avoid trouble | was Jasper's main activity. |
| | *subject* | *predicate* |

---

**PUNCTUATION POINTER**

When an infinitive phrase is the subject of a sentence, no comma is needed.

---

In the spaces provided, write sentences that begin with infinitive phrases. Remember, the subject is the infinitive phrase. The predicate will make the structure a sentence. Study the pattern above before you write.

1. _____

2. _____

3. _____

4. _____

5. _____

Another useful pattern, and a common one, is to add a prepositional phrase between the infinitive phrase and the predicate. The pattern looks like this:

| infinitive phrase | + | prepositional phrase | + | predicate |

A sentence using this pattern, with its parts labeled, is

| To be heard | in a crowded room | is not easy. |
| *infinitive phrase* | *prepositional phrase* | *predicate* |

A few more examples follow, with only the infinitive phrase boxed.

1. | To be a serious student | in school was not so easy.

2. | To have problems | at home didn't appeal to Janice.

3. | To be filled | with hope was normal for the whole street.

4. | To begin | with the speeches was a mistake.

In the spaces below, write short sentences. Begin with an infinitive phrase, follow with a prepositional phrase, end with a predicate. The spaces are labeled as a help.

*Infinitive Phrase*      *Prepositional Phrase*      *Predicate*

1. _____     _____     _____

2. _____     _____     _____

3. _____     _____     _____

4. _____     _____     _____

5. _____     _____     _____

## The infinitive phrase used as a completer

Another common pattern is to use the infinitive phrase as a completer in the predicate. The pattern is:

| subject | + | predicate verb | + | infinitive phrase as completer |

You will recognize some of the examples below as familiar expressions. The infinitive phrases are the first ones we used on page 74. The subject in these examples is unboxed. The predicate verb is underlined. The infinitive phrase as completer is boxed.

1. Jasper <u>wanted</u> to go all the way home.

2. My friend from home <u>wanted</u> to be a playwright.

3. Everybody <u>needs</u> to have enough time.

4. We all <u>decided</u> to decide nothing.

5. The President <u>wants</u> to change the world.

6. Rita <u>knows</u> how to run the office. ["how" is an adverb completer]

7. Jasper <u>tried</u> to begin the meeting.

8. My Uncle Toby <u>doesn't have</u> to give a present.

9. He <u>likes</u> to receive two presents.

10. You <u>should stop</u> to show your pass.

In the blanks below, write short sentences and underline the predicate verb. Leave the subject as is, and box the infinitive phrase used as a completer, as was done above.

1. _____

2. _____

3. _____

4. _____

5. _____

As a final check, study the following sentences. All but one have infinitive phrases in them. Some sentences have more than one infinitive phrase. Put a box around each infinitive phrase you find and be prepared to talk about the way the phrase is used. You should also be able to identify the subject and predicate verb in each sentence.

1. Jasper had to go home for his breakfast.

2. After Rita thought it over, she decided to give it a try.

3. Idomeneo wondered what to do about the mess she was in.

4. To give the secrets to the enemy might be dangerous.

5. No one knew how to keep the blood in the artery.

6. Macky was very sorry, but he had nothing to say about the issues.

7. We plan to give her a promotion in order to keep her here.

8. Rita was elected too late to do anything more this year.

9. To become influential was Bobby's dream.

10. In this town, to want to be mayor was like wanting to be dead.

11. Mr. Panni said it is okay for us to come into his house.

12. Our idea was to move the house over to the pond.

13. Your best bet is to play it close to the vest.

14. We all had to leave early.

15. Did you say anything to Rita?

# principles
# of
# coordination

# 1

## Coordinating Independent Clauses

When structures of the same kind are joined in a sentence, the process is called coordination. We coordinate two independent clauses, two phrases, two subordinate clauses. When two or more independent clauses are joined, a special kind of joiner word is used. It is called a coordinating conjunction.

The main coordinating conjunctions are

> and, or, nor, but, for, yet, so

The pattern for joining two independent clauses together into a sentence is:

| independent clause | + | coordinating conjunction | + |

| independent clause |

In the following sentences both independent clauses are boxed. The word linking them is a coordinating conjunction.

1. | The union wanted to strike, | but | the workers could not agree. |

2. | Your friends are good fun, | and | my friends enjoyed them. |

3. | The idea may be very good, | or | it may be very poor. |

4. | You cannot help him, | for | he refuses to be in anyone's debt. |

5. | Eleazar would not budge, | nor | would he say a word. |

---

**PUNCTUATION POINTER**

A comma follows the first independent clause and comes before the coordinating conjunction. Sometimes it is just as clear to leave the comma out, but only if the independent clauses are very short. The conjunction "nor" always has a comma in front of it, but you will note that the pattern after "nor" is | verb | + | subject |. This is the opposite of the normal pattern after most conjunctions.

---

In the spaces provided below, use each of the seven coordinating conjunctions to join two independent clauses. Box each independent clause, but leave the coordinating conjunction outside the boxes. Try to write the best sentences you can for this exercise. Do not try to write the same independent clauses in each sentence.

1. _____

2. _____

3. _____

4. _____

5. _____

6. _____

7. _____

After you have written the sentences, go over each clause to be sure of two things: (1) that it has both subject and predicate; (2) that it is independent and not subordinate.

**Special paired conjunctions**

Certain conjunctions only work in pairs. Each one introduces its own independent clause. The best-known examples of these are:

> either—or
> neither—nor
> not only—but also

The only problem these conjunctions are likely to give us is the fact that the

$$\boxed{\text{subject}} + \boxed{\text{predicate}}$$

pattern is sometimes reversed, as it is when we

use "nor." Otherwise, the pattern for using these paired conjunctions is

| either | + | independent clause | + | or | + | independent clause |

Some examples of this pattern in action follow. The independent clauses are boxed, but the conjunctions stand alone for easy identification.

1. Either | I go home right away, | or | I stick around here until dinnertime. |

2. Neither | will I praise the Democrats, | nor | will I condemn the Republicans. |

3. Not only | do I have enough money to go to New York, | but | I can also | go to Paris. |

---

**PUNCTUATION POINTER**

The paired coordinating conjunctions use commas to separate them. There is always a comma right before the second conjunction.

---

Use each of the three paired conjunctions in sentences of your own below. Again, try to write the best sentences you can with as much variety as possible.

1. _____

_____

2. _____

_____

3. _____

_____

## The comma splice

Many writers are haunted by the comma splice. It is nothing other than leaving out the coordinating conjunction. Two independent clauses cannot be joined by just a comma. Doing so makes it seem as if two separate sentences have been shoved together. Without a conjunction we don't know what the relationship of the two parts is. The following examples of the comma splice are simply the first five we used earlier, but without the conjunction.

1. The union wanted to strike, the workers could not agree.
2. Your friends are good fun, my friends enjoyed them very much.
3. The idea may be very good, it may be very poor.
4. You cannot help him, he refuses to be in anyone's debt.
5. Eleazar would not budge, he would not say a word.

To see how these examples of the comma splice should be corrected, go back to page 82 and examine their proper form.

Correct the comma splices below, using the best conjunctions you can to make the best sense of the sentence.

1. I have to get the money, I have to pretend to have it.

_____

_____

2. The President was warmly greeted, the crowd seemed delighted to see her.

_____

_____

3. Hank Aaron hit the ball out of the park, it didn't count.

_____

_____

4. You cannot work the problem, I can't work the problem.

_____

_____

5. The labor officials voted yes, the workers voted no.

_____

_____

Go through your own writing for examples of the comma splice. When you find one, write it below. Then rewrite the sentence to correct the comma splice. Check your work carefully to be sure you have a complete sentence.

**Your comma splice:** _____

_____

_____

_____

_____

**Your correction:** _____

_____

_____

_____

# 2

# Coordinating Phrases

When two phrases of the same kind are joined together, we use coordinating conjunctions. Participial phrases, prepositional phrases, and infinitive phrases are all joined to phrases of their own kind by such conjunctions as those boxed below. Note that some are single conjunctions and some are pairs of conjunctions.

> and
> or
> but
> either—or
> neither—nor
> both—and

The pattern for coordinating phrases using one coordinating conjunction is

| phrase | + | coordinating conjunction | + | phrase |

The pattern for the joined pair of coordinating conjunctions is

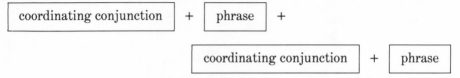

The structures you get from using this method are not sentences. They are parts of a sentence. A phrase lacks either a subject or a predicate, so it cannot be a sentence even if it is linked to another phrase. The way we make these structures into sentences is to join them to a clause. This will be discussed in Section IV, "Principles of Subordination."

### Coordinating participial phrases

Before going on to this section it may help to review pages 65–70, where the participial phrase is discussed in detail.

Study the examples below. The participial phrases are boxed for easy identification, while the coordinating conjunctions stand outside the boxes.

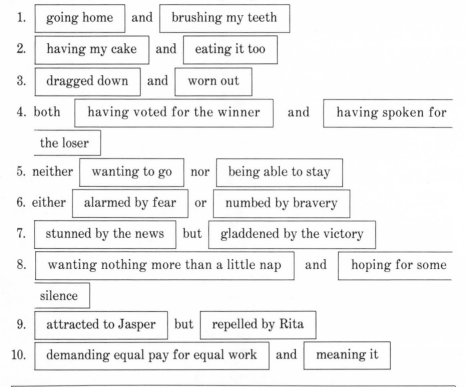

1. going home *and* brushing my teeth
2. having my cake *and* eating it too
3. dragged down *and* worn out
4. both having voted for the winner *and* having spoken for the loser
5. neither wanting to go *nor* being able to stay
6. either alarmed by fear *or* numbed by bravery
7. stunned by the news *but* gladdened by the victory
8. wanting nothing more than a little nap *and* hoping for some silence
9. attracted to Jasper *but* repelled by Rita
10. demanding equal pay for equal work *and* meaning it

---

**PUNCTUATION POINTER**

Commas are not needed between the first phrase and the conjunction. There is always a comma after the second participial phrase when it begins the sentence (see pages 66 and 67), and the subject comes right after the comma.

---

When joining your own participial phrases with conjunctions, both phrases must have the same subject. Some examples of the phrases above turned into sentences might look like this:

1. Attracted to Jasper but repelled by Rita, Joanie  went to the meeting.
      subject      predicate

2. Demanding equal pay for equal work and meaning it, the women
                                                    subject
stuck together.
   predicate

3. Both having voted for the winner and having spoken for the loser,    I
                                                                   subject
was in a touchy situation.
   predicate

You need not write complete sentences in the spaces supplied below. But do write two participial phrases and join them with conjunctions drawn from the examples above. Be sure your phrases are genuine participial phrases and that both of them refer to the same subject. Put a box around each participial phrase, but leave the conjunctions unboxed.

1. _____

_____

2. _____

_____

3. _____

_____

4. _____

_____

5. _____

_____

## Coordinating prepositional phrases

Most of the points mentioned above about linking participial phrases with conjunctions apply to the prepositional phrase, too. The same conjunctions will do the same work. One point to keep in mind is that usually these conjunctions link prepositional phrases that start with the same preposition. Pairs such as these are common:

> with me or with you
> in peace and in war

But the fact is that coordinating conjunctions can link prepositional phrases that start with different prepositions, too. These examples are also common:

> from your friend Alma and with my love
> at home but not in bed

Finally, one of the simplest ways to link prepositional phrases that start with different prepositions is to use *no conjunction at all.* These examples show how easy it is:

> from the halls of Montezuma to the shores of Tripoli
> in enough time for the party
> of more importance to me

Study the examples below. Some use conjunctions, and some do not. The prepositional phrases are boxed.

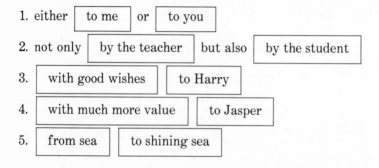

1. either | to me | or | to you |

2. not only | by the teacher | but also | by the student |

3. | with good wishes | | to Harry |

4. | with much more value | | to Jasper |

5. | from sea | | to shining sea |

6. | in a peaceful situation | but | without a real peace |

7. neither | with the President | nor | with the Congress |

8. | with hope | | for the future |

9. | in trouble | | with the law |

10. both | from the U.S. | and | from Russia |

---

**PUNCTUATION POiNTER**

No special punctuation is needed when linking prepositional phrases to one another. Do not use commas here.

---

In the spaces provided below, join your own prepositional phrases, with or without conjunctions from above. Box each prepositional phrase for identification. Be sure to check your work to avoid writing clauses. You do not want both the subject and the predicate here. Review pages 70–73.

1. _____

2. _____

3. _____

4. _____

5. _____

6. _____

7. _____

8. _____

9. _____

10. _____

## Coordinating infinitive phrases

Infinitive phrases can be coordinated with conjunctions or without them. If you wish to review the infinitive phrase before going on to this section, read pages 74–80. The same principles for joining the prepositional phrase apply to the infinitive phrase. The following examples of infinitive phrases coordinated with one another have the phrases boxed for easy identification.

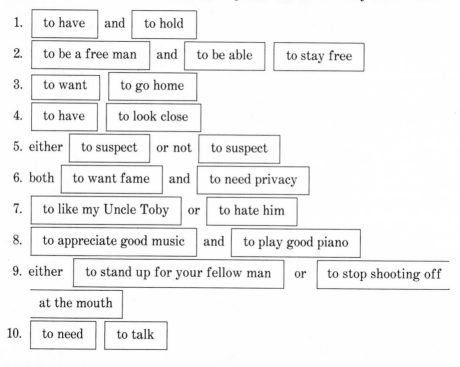

1. to have and to hold

2. to be a free man and to be able to stay free

3. to want to go home

4. to have to look close

5. either to suspect or not to suspect

6. both to want fame and to need privacy

7. to like my Uncle Toby or to hate him

8. to appreciate good music and to play good piano

9. either to stand up for your fellow man or to stop shooting off at the mouth

10. to need to talk

In the spaces provided link your own infinitive phrases. Try as much variety as possible. Use conjunctions for some of your examples; do not use them for others.

1. _____

2. _____

3. _____

4. _____

5. _____

6. _____

7. _____

8. _____

9. _____

10. _____

# Coordinating Subordinate Clauses

Coordinating conjunctions can be used for linking two or more subordinate clauses. They work the same way for subordinate clauses as they do for phrases or for independent clauses. The conjunctions we mentioned—and, or, nor, but, yet—and most of the paired conjunctions work perfectly well for subordinate clauses. The patterns for complete sentences using two subordinate clauses linked together would be:

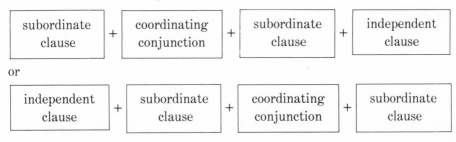

| subordinate clause | + | coordinating conjunction | + | subordinate clause | + | independent clause |

or

| independent clause | + | subordinate clause | + | coordinating conjunction | + | subordinate clause |

As the patterns indicate, the linked subordinate clauses can come either before or after the main clause.

First, let's concentrate on linked subordinate clauses alone. The following examples are not sentences. They lack the independent clause that can make them sentences. They are two subordinate clauses linked with coordinating conjunctions. The subordinate clauses are boxed.

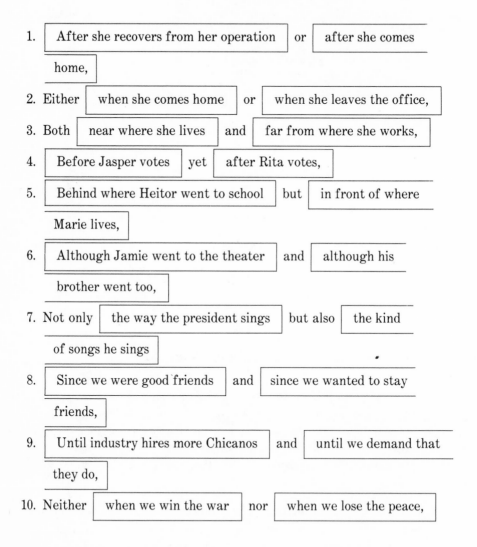

1. | After she recovers from her operation | or | after she comes home, |

2. Either | when she comes home | or | when she leaves the office, |

3. Both | near where she lives | and | far from where she works, |

4. | Before Jasper votes | yet | after Rita votes, |

5. | Behind where Heitor went to school | but | in front of where Marie lives, |

6. | Although Jamie went to the theater | and | although his brother went too, |

7. Not only | the way the president sings | but also | the kind of songs he sings |

8. | Since we were good friends | and | since we wanted to stay friends, |

9. | Until industry hires more Chicanos | and | until we demand that they do, |

10. Neither | when we win the war | nor | when we lose the peace, |

These fragments all begin with a capital letter to show that they are frequently used to begin sentences. They have no end punctuation because they must be linked to independent clauses before they can be sentences.

Before doing the following exercise, review in Section II, Unit 2, "The Subordinate Clause," pages 59–65. Once you have done that, supply examples of your own subordinate clauses linked by coordinate conjunctions in the spaces provided. Be sure to box each subordinate clause for ready identification.

1. _____

2. _____

3. _____

4. _____

5. _____

6. _____

7. _____

8. _____

9. _____

10. _____

## Writing complete sentences using linked subordinate clauses

The patterns at the beginning of this unit (page 93) show how to make complete sentences using linked subordinate clauses. The sentence can either start with the independent clause or end with it. The sentences below illustrate both patterns. The independent clause is underlined and the subordinate clauses are boxed in both examples. Both examples are equally correct. The paired conjunctions are "either" or "or."

<u>Blood Sweat and Tears will play something</u> either | before the boogie group comes out | or | after Sha Na Na plays. |

Either | before the boogie group comes out | or | after Sha Na Na plays, | <u>Blood Sweat and Tears will play something.</u>

Several more examples follow. In each the independent clause is underlined and the subordinate clauses are boxed. The conjunctions stand alone. Study the examples carefully.

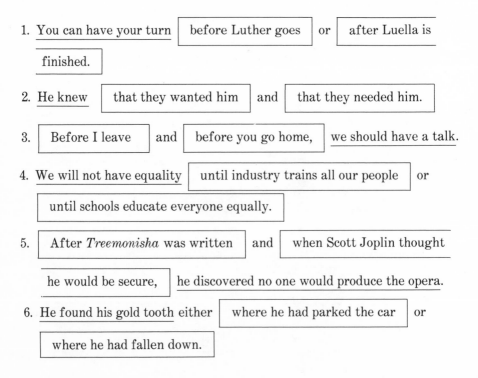

1. <u>You can have your turn</u> | before Luther goes | or | after Luella is finished. |

2. <u>He knew</u> | that they wanted him | and | that they needed him. |

3. | Before I leave | and | before you go home, | <u>we should have a talk.</u>

4. <u>We will not have equality</u> | until industry trains all our people | or | until schools educate everyone equally. |

5. | After *Treemonisha* was written | and | when Scott Joplin thought he would be secure, | <u>he discovered no one would produce the opera.</u>

6. <u>He found his gold tooth</u> either | where he had parked the car | or | where he had fallen down. |

Make your own sentences below with linked subordinate clauses and an independent clause. Underline your independent clause whether it begins the sentence or ends it. Box both your subordinate clauses, and leave your conjunctions unmarked. You may use the linked subordinate clauses from your previous exercise.

1. _____

_____

2. _____

_____

3. _____

_____

4. _____

_____

5. _____

_____

---

**COMPOSITION POINTER**

Find at least one example in your writing where you linked two subordinate clauses in a sentence. Write it below. Then, in the second section, try to improve your first effort.

**Your example of linked subordinate clauses from your work:**

_____

_____

_____

**Your example improved:** _____

_____

_____

_____

_____

---

# principles
# of
# subordination

# 1

# Subordinating Clauses: Time and Place

When we talk about subordinating clauses, we are talking about linking them to independent clauses. If we can say that the independent clause has the main information or the main idea of the sentence, then the subordinate clause helps clarify that idea. The subordinate clause gives important information or description which makes the independent clause clearer and more complete. Whenever we consider linking subordinate clauses to independent clauses, we can use one of the two patterns that follow:

| subordinate clause, | + | independent clause |

or

| independent clause | + | subordinate clause |

All of the subordinate clauses we discuss in this section will follow the patterns above.

The special kind of subordinate clause in this unit clarifies or describes time or place. It begins with subordinators answering questions about when or where something happened or will happen. You have already seen some examples of these in Section II, Unit 2, "The Subordinate Clause." The examples below are subordinate clauses that give us information about time or place.

**Subordinators of time:**

| 1. now when | 8. when |
| 2. after | 9. whenever |
| 3. before | 10. while |
| 4. until | 11. _____ |
| 5. during the time when | 12. _____ |
| 6. always when | 13. _____ |
| 7. as soon as | 14. _____ |

Study the list above very carefully. These words are the main subordinators of time in our language. The following examples all begin with subordinators of time:

1. After we went home
2. When everyone cheered the President
3. As soon as Rita kissed Jasper

4. While Hilda and Margot waited nearby
5. Until the word was passed to the people
6. Before any vote was taken
7. During the time when Zaire was called the Belgian Congo
8. Whenever we go to Mexico
9. Twenty days before he sent for the chief
10. Now when we need him

| Subordinators of place: | |
|---|---|
| 1. where | 8. close to where |
| 2. under where | 9. toward where |
| 3. near where | 10. from wherever |
| 4. next to where | 11. _____ |
| 5. wherever | 12. _____ |
| 6. behind where | 13. _____ |
| 7. there where | 14. _____ |

These examples begin with subordinators of place.

1. Near where I live
2. Next to where Louie's bar and grill used to be
3. Where Iris and Jacinto held their debate
4. Under where she signed her name
5. There where Madeleine was standing
6. Wherever I go
7. Above the apartment where I live
8. Wherever the President stands
9. Where the Republic of China meets India
10. From where I was sitting

---

**POINTER**

The subordinate clause of place has one main subordinator: "where." "Wherever" is also useful, but not as useful as "where." The examples of subordinate clauses of time and place given above may seem easy enough when you look at them. However, they are tricky. Be sure that when you write your own examples of subordinate clauses, you avoid writing phrases. Be sure your clauses have both subject and predicate. But even more important, be sure you have not written an independent clause whose predicate has an adverb completer of time or place. We discussed such structures in Section I, Unit 4, "The Predicate with Adverb Completers." Go over your work to be sure you have a clause that is not a complete sentence.

---

Using some of the subordinators above, write your own subordinate clauses of time and of place.

1. _____

2. _____

3. _____

4. _____

5. _____

6. _____

7. _____

8. _____

9. _____

10. _____

## Using subordinate clauses of time in a sentence

Any of your subordinate clauses of time above can be made into sentences by linking them to independent clauses. As we said at first, the independent clause can come at the beginning or at the end of the sentence. Both ways are equally good. Sometimes the meaning of the sentence is slightly altered when the subordinate clause comes first. Here is an example of a sentence whose meaning changes depending on where the subordinate clause comes. The independent clause is underlined and the subordinate clause is boxed. Examine both versions:

1. José was determined to go to law school | after he finished college.

2. | After he finished college, | José was determined to go to law school.

In sentence 1 it seems clear that José has not yet finished college, but in sentence 2 it seems that he had already finished college when he decided on law school. The shift in meaning is a result of placing the subordinate clause before the main clause.

<br>

**PUNCTUATION POINTER**

When the subordinate clause of time begins the sentence, a comma follows it. No comma is used when the subordinate clause of time comes after the independent clause.

<br>

The following examples are complete sentences using subordinate clauses of time. Some of the sentences begin with the subordinate clause and some end with the subordinate clause. In each case the independent clause is underlined and the subordinate clause of time is boxed for ready identification.

1. The Congress reconsidered the measure | after the President vetoed it. |

2. No one dared make a move | until the robbers left the bank. |

3. | When everyone had gone, | Jasper closed the hall.

4. | From the time when we were little, | our parents made their own wine.

5. The assembly shouted approval | when Rita told them what she had done. |

6. | Always when she had done such a thing, | Moira would tell us right away.

7. The children played in the sandbox | while the rockets shot overhead. |

8. | During the time when they were fighting, | we hid across the street.

9. No one wanted him | now that he was not the champ anymore.

10. | As soon as we found out about it, | we decided to take action.

In the spaces below, write your own complete sentences using a subordinate clause of time. Make some of the sentences begin with the subordinate clause and some with the independent clause. Be sure to use proper punctuation. Make a box around the subordinate clause.

1. _____

2. _____

3. _____

4. _____

5. _____

**COMPOSITION POINTER**

Go through a recent essay and see if you have a sentence or a group of sentences that could have been improved by using a subordinate clause of time. Look for an example that used more words than necessary or that was not as clear as it should have been. Write the sentence or sentences in the first section below. Then write an improved version in the second section provided below.

**Your example from your writing:** _____

_____

_____

_____

**Your improvement using a subordinate clause of time:** _____

_____

_____

_____

_____


## Using subordinate clauses of place in a sentence

Since the subordinate clause of place can come first or last in a sentence, the patterns we will use will look like this:

| subordinate clause of place, | + | independent clause |

or

| independent clause | + | subordinate clause of place |

In the example that follows, the same subordinate clause of place and the same independent clause are arranged both ways. Examine them for any difference in meaning. The independent clause is underlined and the subordinate clause of place is boxed in each example for easy identification.

1. Near where José lives, I used to visit my girlfriend.

2. I used to visit my girlfriend near where José lives.

---

**PUNCTUATION POINTER**

As you can see, when the subordinate clause of place comes first in the sentence, it is followed by a comma. No comma is used when the subordinate clause of place comes last in the sentence. There is an

---

exception. In the examples following, you may notice that sometimes the independent clause has this pattern:

| predicate verb | + | subject | + | completers |

This happens when the subordinate clause of place comes first and is followed by a form of the verb "to be." Here is an example of that situation with the parts boxed and labeled.

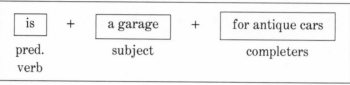

Behind where my Uncle Toby works

subordinate clause of place

| is | + | a garage | + | for antique cars |
| pred. verb | | subject | | completers |

independent clause

No comma is needed in this example even though the subordinate clause comes first.

All the examples below have the independent clause underlined and the subordinate clause of place boxed for identification.

1. There was a beautiful beam of sunshine where Madeleine was standing.

2. Where the river flows to the sea is a temple for Buddhist priests.

3. The boundaries of the republic ended where the great desert began.

4. Wherever she signed her name, Gladys put her thumbprint.

5. I wanted to be where Yolande was.

6. We were stranded where the reef juts out of the sea.

7. Wherever people get together, we will always have friends.

8. Near where we spotted the island of St. Helena, we tried to make radio contact with you.

9. I saw you | where the bus stops in the morning.

10. The Congressman moved | next to where I stood.

Write your own complete sentences below, using subordinate clauses of place. Either begin or end your sentences with the subordinate clause, and be sure to box it for identification. Aim for as much variety in your choice of subordinators as possible. You may use any of the subordinators listed in this unit. You may also use other subordinators if you think of some.

1. _____

2. _____

3. _____

4. _____

5. _____

---

**COMPOSITION POINTER**

Go through a recent sample of your own writing and find a sentence or two in which you needed a subordinate clause of place but didn't use one. Write that sentence or those sentences in the first section below. Then rewrite the sentences using a subordinate clause of place in the second section provided below.

**Your example from your writing:** _____

_____

_____

_____

**Your improvement using a subordinate clause of place:** _____

_____

_____

_____

_____

# Subordinating Clauses: Action

Many subordinate clauses give information about the way things are done. Some give information about the causes of actions or even the limits of actions. They can give information about the how, the why, and the result of actions described in the independent clause. Not every different kind of clause describing action needs to be named, but if you examine the list of typical subordinators which follows, you can see how they help point toward their function. Each subordinator in the list is linked to a clause in the examples which follow.

| | |
|---|---|
| 1. as if | 11. unless |
| 2. as | 12. supposing that |
| 3. as though | 13. provided that |
| 4. because | 14. even |
| 5. since | 15. even though |
| 6. so | 16. although |
| 7. so that | 17. while |
| 8. in order that | 18. _____ |
| 9. if | 19. _____ |
| 10. even if | 20. _____ |

The last three blank spaces are for you to fill in. There are many more subordinators that do the job of telling why, how, and what happens if an action is committed. You will discover them as you read and as you write. The patterns for punctuation with these subordinate clauses is the same as those we have already examined:

| subordinate clause | + | , | + | independent clause |

or

| independent clause | + | subordinate clause |

Examine these examples using the subordinators above. The subordinate clause in each example is boxed for easy identification.

1. Rita acted | as if Jasper did not have a vote. |

2. | As we learned later, | the money had been taken before we got there.

3. He winked at me | as he boarded the plane. |

4. The President acted | as though nothing had happened. |

5. | Because we were totally fed up with him, | we just left early.

6. Everyone loves Rita | because she is so cheerful. |

7. | Since you went back to school, | they rented your room to me.

8. They wanted us to meet tonight | since tomorrow is likely to be too late. |

9. We did not know what to do | so we went home instead of going to the movies. |

10. Louis spoke quietly | so that none of us would get scared. |

11. | In order that everyone could get in on time, | Jim pulled a fast one.

12. | If you want to be a serious politician, | you will have to study history.

13. They will not come here | if no one wants them. |

14. | Even if you confess, | we will not grant you a lighter sentence.

15. | Unless something happens soon, | this place is going to blow up.

16. | Supposing that we play early, | I can get home before dark.

17. Arthur Ashe will play tennis against Jimmy Connors | provided that they repair the court. |

18. | Even though you like what you do, | you might want to try a change.

19. | Although Louella was a liberated woman, | Piquay pretended not to notice.

20. | While I do not dislike you, | I cannot say I think you're terrific.

---

**PUNCTUATION POINTER**

There are times when you will want to use a comma between the independent and subordinate clauses even when the subordinate clause comes last. In sentences 8 and 17 above, some writers would use a comma to indicate a pause. This is not incorrect and would not cause trouble with clarity.

---

One subordinator we did not list is "like." It often substitutes for "as." Be careful in using "like" to be sure it means "as" in the sentences you write. In conversation, "like" is usually clear. We can be understood saying, "like Jasper used to say," "like people were not hungry enough," "like Rita might have been hurt." But "like" does not work as well in writing unless it has the same meaning as "as" or "as if." Using "like" cautiously will save problems in clarity.

In the spaces provided below, write ten sentences using ten different subordinators from the list above. Aim at as much variety as possible. Put some of the subordinate clauses first in the sentence and some second. Be sure your sentences make good sense.

1. _____

2. _____

3. _____

4. _____

5. _____

6. _____

7. _____

8. _____

9. _____

10. _____

---

**COMPOSITION POINTER**

Examine some of your recent writing for examples of the subordinators of action listed above. Find some subordinate clauses using these subordinators and write them below.

**Your sentence with a subordinate clause of action:** _____

_____

_____

_____

_____

_____

**Your sentence with a subordinate clause of action:** _____

_____

_____

_____

_____

# Subordinating Clauses: People and Things

Subordinate clauses often give more detailed information about who or what something is. The independent clause will sometimes refer to a person or a thing without giving as much detail as is needed for a reader to understand the reference. When this happens, one easy way of making the reference clear is to add a subordinate clause naming the person or thing. This kind of clause can come at the beginning or end of the sentence, and it can also come right in the middle. It can literally interrupt the independent clause and come between its subject and verb. The patterns one uses most often are illustrated here:

1. | Whoever told him to come in | + | was pretty nervy. |

          subordinate clause           predicate verb
          used as subject           and completer

2. | Jimmy was a person | + | whom everyone loved. |

          independent           subordinate
          clause           clause

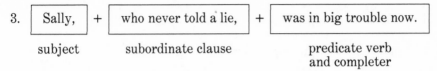

| Sally, | + | who never told a lie, | + | was in big trouble now. |
|---|---|---|---|---|
| subject | | subordinate clause | | predicate verb and completer |

Each of these examples is somewhat different. All refer to people, though as the examples will show, they could also refer to things and ideas. They name and/or describe people in such a way that they can be better understood. In example 1, the subordinate clause is actually part of the independent clause. This pattern is one we have not fully discussed before, so it may be tricky at first. Subordinate clauses can be used as either a subject or as a completer of the predicate verb. The examples that follow show the patterns which are most common when the subordinate clause is used as part of the independent clause. Each of the examples is an independent clause used as a sentence. Each subordinate clause is boxed and identified as either subject or completer of a predicate verb.

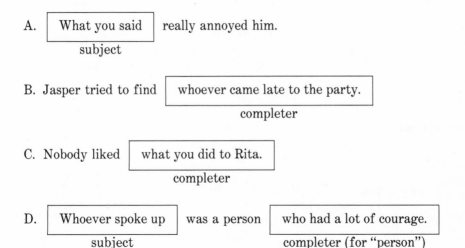

A. [ What you said ] really annoyed him.
   subject

B. Jasper tried to find [ whoever came late to the party. ]
   completer

C. Nobody liked [ what you did to Rita. ]
   completer

D. [ Whoever spoke up ] was a person [ who had a lot of courage. ]
   subject                              completer (for "person")

The last of these examples combines the use of the subordinate clause as a subject with the subordinate clause added to the end of the independent clause.

The examples which follow are based on the patterns described above. In each case, the subordinate clause is boxed for easy identification.

1. [ Whatever you did ] made him furious.

2. Nobody [ who was anybody ] was there.

3. [ Whoever tried to break into the cafe ] made off with the key.

4. | Whoever spoke up | was the one they were looking for.

5. The president was the man | who could never tell a lie.

6. Margaret is a girl | who can size up a situation fast.

7. The Cordozas are people | whom we always see at parties.

8. Rita had a hat | that made her look smashing.

9. Magritte knew | which wall should be painted white.

10. Franco Harris is an athlete | who excells in many sports.

11. My Uncle Toby, | who went to Australia, | is coming home.

12. He saw Jimmy Breen, | who had that accident near Tunbridge Wells.

13. Fishing, | which is not the national sport, | can be very relaxing.

14. That idea, | whose time has not quite come, | is a dead issue now.

15. My mother, | who would never say such a thing, | was shocked.

16. The man | who told me how to get there | was lost.

17. I saw the girl | who had no eye teeth | order a hero sandwich.

18. Jimmy was a friend | who needed help.

19. People | who need people | are the luckiest people.

20. The folks | who know good cooking | go to Lucille's for dinner.

---

**PUNCTUATION POINTER**

You will notice that sentences 11–15 use commas to separate the subordinate clause from the rest of the sentence. Sentences 16–20 do not use commas. The reason is very important. The first kind of clause (that in sentences 11–15) is called non-restrictive. The second kind of clause is called restrictive. Non-restrictive clauses do not identify the person or thing named any more clearly than the word or words that precede the clause. In other words, a non-restrictive clause adds more information about the word it refers to, but it is only additional, not absolutely critical, information.

The restrictive clause identifies the word or words it refers to and limits it from all other things of its kind. Sentence 20 is a case in point. What kind of folks go to Lucille's? Those who know good cooking. This clause restricts the meaning of "folks" to a certain group. Therefore it does not need commas.

One way to remember this difference is that the non-restrictive clause is almost an interruption and needs commas to signal its beginning and end. The restrictive clause gives crucial information and is of first importance to understanding the sentence. *Remember: if the information the clause gives is of crucial importance to understanding the sentence, leave out the commas. If the information the clause gives can be left out without changing the meaning of the sentence, then use commas around it.* In sentences 16–20, all the restrictive clauses could be left out, but there would be no way to know what man, what girl, what friend, what people, or what folks the sentences were talking about. The restrictive clause gives crucial information that cannot be done without.

In the following spaces write ten sentences using subordinate clauses naming persons, things, or ideas. Be sure to write some sentences using restrictive clauses and some using non-restrictive clauses. Refer to the models before trying your own sentences.

1. _____

2. _____

3. _____

4. _____

5. _____

6. _____

7. _____

8. _____

9. _____

10. _____

---

**COMPOSITION POINTER**

Go through some of your recent writing and find an example of a subordinate clause naming persons, things, or ideas. Write it in the space below.

**Your sentence with a subordinate clause naming a person, thing, or idea:**

_____

_____

_____

_____

If you feel your example is a good one, properly punctuated, leave it as is. If you feel you can improve upon it, do so in the space provided below.

**Your sentence improved:** _____

_____

_____

_____

_____

In the spaces below, write all the typical subordinators of clauses naming person, things, and ideas. See if you can add to the subordinators used in the examples.

1. _____     9. _____

2. _____     10. _____

3. _____     11. _____

4. _____     12. _____

5. _____     13. _____

6. _____     14. _____

7. _____     15. _____

8. _____

# Subordinating Phrases

Just as subordinate clauses are linked to independent clauses, phrases can be linked to both independent and subordinate clauses. The same subordinators can start phrases as well as clauses. The same kinds of subordinate phrases can be written as well as clauses. We are going to emphasize the kinds of phrases listed below. Many of the same points discussed about subordinate clauses will be discussed about subordinate phrases.

> phrases of time
> phrases of place
> phrases of manner
> phrases of cause

Most of the phrases in this unit are prepositional phrases which begin with adverb prepositions. It would be useful to review Section II, Unit 4, "The Prepositional Phrase," before going further here. Other kinds of phrases, such as the participial and the infinitive, can be linked together with prepositional phrases to make a phrase of time or place. An example of this would be

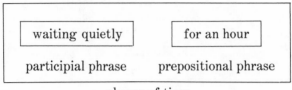

phrase of time

Structures of this kind will appear often in this unit. But there is no need to break each phrase down into its parts. Instead, spend your energy on deciding whether a phrase concerns itself with time, place, cause, or manner. Spend your energy equally on writing clear phrases and good phrases.

The pattern for using these phrases in a sentence could be any one of the following:

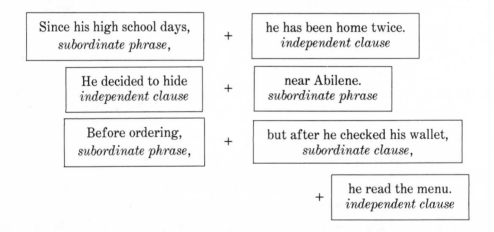

Actually, many variations of the three parts in the last example can make a good sentence. The subordinate phrase can usually come anywhere in the sentence.

## Phrases of time

Some typical phrases of time appear below linked to an independent clause. It would be just as possible to include a subordinate clause with any of these sentences. But for clarity we will not make things more difficult than they need be. The phrase of time is boxed and the independent clause is underlined.

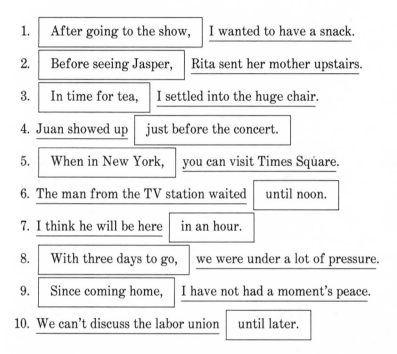

1. After going to the show, | I wanted to have a snack.

2. Before seeing Jasper, | Rita sent her mother upstairs.

3. In time for tea, | I settled into the huge chair.

4. Juan showed up | just before the concert.

5. When in New York, | you can visit Times Square.

6. The man from the TV station waited | until noon.

7. I think he will be here | in an hour.

8. With three days to go, | we were under a lot of pressure.

9. Since coming home, | I have not had a moment's peace.

10. We can't discuss the labor union | until later.

The subordinators used here, "after," "before," "in," "with," "when," "since," and "until," should be familiar by now. If you would like to review a list of subordinators of time, see page 100 of Section IV, Unit 1, "Subordinating Clauses: Time and Place." In the spaces below supply your own sentences using phrases of time. Box the phrase of time and underline the independent clause.

1. _____

2. _____

3. _____

4. _____

5. _____

6. _____

7. _____

8. _____

9. _____

10. _____

## Phrases of place

The examples below are typical phrases of place linked to independent clauses. The phrase of place begins with a subordinator of place such as those listed on page 18 in Section I, Unit 4, "The Predicate with Adverb Completers." You may wish to review those before doing your own sentences later. The subordinators of place on page 101 are really useful only for clauses, so do not use them.

1. | Near Henry | is a girl I want you to meet.

2. I don't think anyone wants to be | close to a machine gun. |

3. | Next to the old movie house | Fred set up shop.

4. | Behind the First National Bank | Jim found a bag with silver dollars in it.

5. Jasper kept his books | on the shelf | | beside the fireplace. |

6. | In the bag | | next to the window | is a cup of coffee.

7. The horse ran | across the river | and | into the trees. |

8. The President had an interview | by the Washington Monument. |

9. | Out back of the playground | is a beautiful trout stream.

10. Sammy hit the ball | just left of first base. |

These phrases can be thought of as completers of place in the sentence, just as we described the adverb completer of place on pages 18–19. You will note from examples 5, 6, and 7 that phrases of place can be linked together one after the other to get a more exact sense of place.

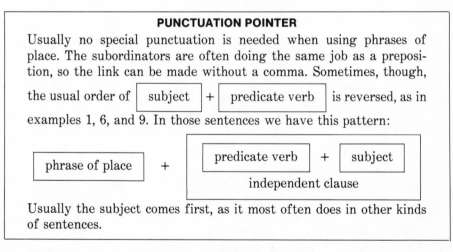

**PUNCTUATION POINTER**

Usually no special punctuation is needed when using phrases of place. The subordinators are often doing the same job as a preposition, so the link can be made without a comma. Sometimes, though, the usual order of | subject | + | predicate verb | is reversed, as in examples 1, 6, and 9. In those sentences we have this pattern:

| phrase of place | + | predicate verb | + | subject |
    independent clause

Usually the subject comes first, as it most often does in other kinds of sentences.

Write your own short sentences below using phrases of place. Be sure to avoid writing clauses of place by checking to see that you do not have both subject and predicate. Be sure, too, that your independent clause is really an independent clause by checking it carefully. Box the phrases of place used here and underline your independent clauses.

1. _____

2. _____

3. _____

4. _____

5. _____

6. _____

7. _____

8. _____

9. _____

10. _____


**Phrases of manner**

The phrase of manner is often a prepositional phrase that gives information about how something is done. It usually begins with a special completer of manner such as "as though," "as if," "as," "in the manner of," "as fast as," and some of those used on pages 20 and 21, when we first spoke about completers of manner. The phrase of manner tells us something about the "how" of the clause to which it is attached.

The examples of phrases of manner below are clearly linked to an independent clause to make a sentence. The phrase completes the sense of the independent clause by telling us some important information. When you discuss these examples, decide what that information really is.

1. | By studying hard, | we can begin to understand the language.

2. He stood by | as if shocked by the news.

3. | As though amused at my pain, | the conductor smiled and left.

4. | As if stunned by the news, | Sharon let herself fall into the chair.

5. Manny was quiet | as a church mouse.

6. He ran | as fast as a gazelle.

7. Luther was acting | as if guilty.

8. The President took part | as a host.

9. | As though amused at the thought of it, | Larry let the opportunity go.

10. | As a friend in need, | Toby was not much good.

---

**PUNCTUATION POINTER**

We are back now to the original pattern of using a comma when the phrase of manner comes before the independent clause. No comma is used when the phrase of manner comes after the independent clause.

---

One thing to notice about these phrases is that examples 1, 2, 3, 4, and 9 are participial phrases beginning with subordinators of manner. You can make a phrase of manner out of almost any participial phrase by simply starting with a subordinator of manner. The other examples above are subordinators of manner completed by a word that could be a simple subject. In examples 5–8 "church mouse," "gazelle," "host," and even "guilty" are the names of a thing or a state of mind. Reviewing Section I, Unit 1, "The Simple Subject," will bring some of those words back to mind.

The patterns for these phrases can be the following:

| subordinator of manner | + | participial phrase |

or

| subordinator of manner | + | naming word or phrase |

In the patterns above, the subordinator of manner is doing the job of an adverb completer and a preposition, so we sometimes call them prepositional adverbs.

Write your own sentences below using the phrase of manner linked to an independent clause. Underline the independent clause and box the phrase of manner. Be careful to follow the instructions above for structuring the phrase of manner.

1. _____

2. _____

3. _____

4. _____

5. _____

6. _____

7. _____

8. _____

9. _____

10. _____

## Phrases of cause

The structure for phrases of cause is like that of the phrase of manner. The main subordinators of cause are "because," "because of," and any other word or words that mean "because." Both the patterns below can make phrases of cause, but the first pattern is by far the more common one:

| subordinator of cause | + | naming word or phrase |

or

| subordinator of cause | + | participial phrase |

Again, the subordinator of cause is usually doing the job of the adverb completer and a preposition.

The phrase of cause can come first or last in a sentence. When it comes before the independent clause, a comma links it to that clause. No comma is used if the phrase of cause comes after the independent clause.

1. | Because of his meanness, | Freddy was often left out of the fun.

2. The picnic was cancelled | on account of rain. |

3. | On account of the cost, | Jamie could not treat his friends.

4. | By being home today, | Luella was able to take the call herself.

5. The republic was saved | because of the commander's quick thinking. |

6. | Because of his military skill, | Washington was asked to be President.

7. | Because of his illness, | he was sent to the hospital.

8. Felipe was saddened | because of the bad news. |

9. Sandy and his neighbor stayed together | because of the dark. |

10. He was given preference | on account of his name. |

Following the patterns above, write your own brief sentences below. Try to get as much variety into your sentences as possible. Be sure to write phrases and not clauses of cause. Underline the main clause and box the phrase of cause.

1. _____

2. _____

3. _____

4. _____

5. _____

6. _____

7. _____

8. _____

9. _____

10. _____

---

**COMPOSITION POINTER**

Go through your recent writing and try to find sentences which include one of the four kinds of phrases we have been discussing. Write them in the boxes below. Do you feel your uses of these phrases are good? If not, rewrite some to improve them.

**Your phrase of time in a sentence:** _____

_____

_____

_____

_____

_____

_____

**Your phrase of place in a sentence:** _____

_____

_____

_____

_____

_____

_____

**Your phrase of manner in a sentence:** _____

_____

_____

_____

_____

_____

_____

**Your phrase of cause in a sentence:** _____

_____

_____

_____

_____

_____

_____

If you should find none of these in your writing, be sure to include some in your next essay. When you do, fill in the boxes above from your new writing.

# achieving
# variety

# 1

# Simplifying Sentences

The only reason for learning the structures or patterns of various sentences is to use them. Once they are learned you should use them consciously to improve your writing, even in the first-draft stage. Most of what appears in this part of the book is helpful for rewriting, a process most good writers go through for hours on end.

One basic trouble in most people's writing is the fact that they often get lost in the sentence. They write sentences that are much too long and much too unclear. The structures which are there for all of us to use somehow don't get used. Instead of using a snappy phrase of time, people let themselves wander into a long clause of time. Instead of putting a phrase or clause where it will do the most good, they sometimes let it get buried in the middle of a sentence where its importance is not clear.

What this means is that since almost all writers tend to write long, vague, and sometimes much too fancy sentences, everyone can use some instruction in how to simplify a long sentence. This is getting back to the basics. It is using basic sentence structure and what we know of it to examine the long sentences we write to see how to make them better. The examples that follow were all written by students just beginning college. The kinds of problems they have are shared by almost every beginning writer.

### Looking for the major parts in a long sentence

Not all long sentences are problems, but when one becomes a problem, it is important to know how to break it down to its parts so it can be rebuilt again. The following sentence has its parts badly organized:

> The fact that he broke his ankle helped to teach him a lesson because he would have to depend on his father to help him, even though Mike felt ashamed of his father.

Most of us would probably be able to make some sense out of this sentence. Its parts are not clearly organized, though. If we look closely we can break its parts down in this way:

> 1. the fact that breaking his ankle taught him a lesson
> 2. the causal relationship with his father's help
> 3. the "even though" clause

Nothing is really clear in this sentence. How does the broken ankle teach him a lesson? What is the lesson? One way of clearing things up could be

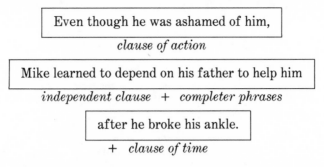

Here the clause of action does some of the work of a clause of cause, so we do not need a separate structure talking about cause. The independent clause has this structure:

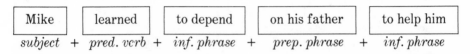

It is not necessary to break down all sentences this far, but it sometimes helps. The sentence as it is rewritten is clearer than before, but will need other sentences to explain what is not discussed here (for example, the fact that this experience taught him a lesson).

Another example from a student essay is below. It is even more formless than the one above. It does not try to set up clauses of cause or action. It simply rambles on, adding one thing to the next with no reason for their connection:

> While reading the early half of the story, questions rose in my mind as to whether or not the joining forces of Sergeant Tree's ever-growing sly and contemptuous mind would unite with Bung's hulkish strength to overthrow Hawkins.

This is not a clear sentence. What we have to do is look closely at what is here and list its most important parts:

1. phrase of time about reactions early in the story
2. question about whether Sergeant Tree will join forces with Bung to overthrow Hawkins

The problems of the sentence have to do with time and the qualities Bung and Tree bring together. Straightening those problems out is not as tough as it seems at first. Here is one solution:

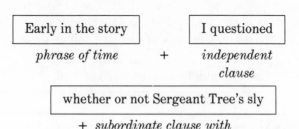

Early in the story · I questioned

*phrase of time* + *independent clause*

whether or not Sergeant Tree's sly

+ *subordinate clause with*

and contemptuous mind would unite with Bung's hulkish strength

*completers*

to overthrow Hawkins.

+ *infinitive phrase*

Now the major ideas in this sentence are clearly related. Again, other sentences in the essay might explain about Sergeant Tree's mind or Bung's strength. We would also like to know about Hawkins. Is he the good guy or the bad guy? Many questions remain.

In the examples above, the number of words in the improved version is smaller than in the original version. The first sentence has 33 words in the original version but only 22 words in the improved version. The second sentence is reduced from 39 words (counting "ever-growing" as two words) to 24 words. This kind of reduction is what you should aim at not only in the examples that follow, but in your own writing.

In the following examples try a step-by-step approach to each sentence. Your job is to use fewer words in the improved version. It is even more important that you write a clearer sentence in your improved version. The following checklist will help you. Follow it carefully as you do each sentence.

---

**RULES FOR SIMPLIFICATION**

1. Circle the major ideas or parts of the sentence. Write them in the space labeled **Major parts**.
2. Decide what is of most importance. Check it and use it in your independent clause.
3. If two parts are of equal value, decide how to coordinate them.
4. Decide what kinds of subordinate clauses or phrases will be necessary for each of the other parts. If necessary, try several kinds until you get the right one.
5. Review the kinds of subordination available to you. If you are in doubt about which kind to use, see if the parts of the sentence do or should answer questions about time, place, manner, cause. If parts in your sample do not seem related to any of these questions, try to make them relate by rewriting the sentence.

---

All of the following examples are from student essays. All need to be simplified and made clearer.

1. The gentleness and affection he showed this young girl and quite similarly to the Dean woman, proved he was capable of being what we would consider quite normal and he would be functioning quite well in America.

**Major parts:** _____

_____

_____

_____

_____

**Your simplification:** _____

_____

_____

_____

_____

2. On a Friday night I was in the town of New York where I reside with a few of my friends.

**Major parts:** _____

_____

_____

_____

**Your simplification:** _____

_____

_____

_____

3. I'll never forget the time I was so drunk that I fell into the bathtub and none of my friends would help me up so I just lay there a while and after about ten minutes they decided to help me up.

**Major parts:** _____

_____

_____

_____

**Your simplification:** _____

_____

_____

_____

4. It sounds like he is talking about his inner self his own consciousness, his innermost part of his mind or he could be just talking about his self in general, in a way showing his own self as he really is, in his own eyes.

**Major parts:** _____

_____

_____

_____

_____

**Your simplification:** _____

_____

_____

_____

_____

5. He is in a world of bondage because these people pay no attention to him, it's like being in a cage, isolated from everything.

**Major parts:** _____

_____

_____

_____

_____

**Your simplification:** _____

_____

_____

_____

_____

Revising someone else's writing is always helpful. However, it is even more important to learn to revise your own writing. Most beginning writers simply do not bother to revise. Most professional writers revise all the time. The work you did in the exercises above should help prepare you to learn how to revise and improve your own sentences. If you have not tried to do any revision before, you will be surprised at how much improvement you can make in a short time.

Go through your own writing looking for examples of sentences that need simplification. If necessary, ask your teacher to point out sentences that need to be improved and simplified. Write them in the first section provided. Then list their major parts in the second section. Your improved version should go in the third section. You might also try this with a sentence from someone else in your group. It helps some writers to see how a friend can revise what he writes. Be sure to follow the rules for simplification on page 132.

**1. Your original sentence:** _____

_____

_____

**Major parts:** _____

_____

_____

_____

**Your simplification:** _____

_____

_____

_____

2. **Your original sentence:** _____

_____

_____

_____

**Major parts:** _____

_____

_____

_____

_____

_____

**Your simplification:** _____

_____

_____

_____

3.  **Your original sentence:** _____

_____

_____

_____

**Major parts:** _____

_____

_____

_____

**Your simplification:** _____

_____

_____

_____

_____

4. Your original sentence: _____

_____

_____

_____

Major parts: _____

_____

_____

_____

Your simplification: _____

_____

_____

_____

_____

**5. Your original sentence:** _____

_____

_____

_____

**Major parts:** _____

_____

_____

_____

**Your simplification:** _____

_____

_____

_____

# 2
# Varying Sentence Length

Variety is essential in writing. In direct speech, we change the tone or volume of sound as well as the patterns of our sentences. We also need variety in our writing because it helps maintain the attention of our audience. Its absence might cause us to lose an audience even if what we have to say is worthwhile. Therefore, knowing how to write sentences of a single clause, or of coordinated independent clauses, or clauses subordinated to independent clauses, is essential for achieving variety in writing.

Naturally, some variety is essential, but we should not overdo things by making variety our only object and goal. There is no reason to demand that every sentence be different from the one before it or the one after it. Our goal, then, is to achieve *some* variety when we want it.

One reason to think consciously about variety is the fact that most writers pay no attention to it. Very often beginning writers go to one of two extremes. The first is very common: writing sentences that are much too long and badly organized. Some of these sentences appeared in the previous unit, "Simplifying Sentences." The other extreme is that of writing very short, choppy sentences which often begin with the same word or kind of word and which almost never have any subordinate clauses or subordinate phrases. These are the extremes, and you will probably recognize one or the other of these as a problem you sometimes have. If you have had a paper come back to you marked "run-on sentence" or "choppy, awkward," you can be sure you have had these problems. The way to avoid these problems is to know about them and then work either to rewrite later or to vary your sentence structures as you write. Either way will produce the desired results: putting some balance into your writing through varying the sentence length.

## Working with choppy sentences

Our last section on simplification dealt with sentences that were too long and unclear. This section will concentrate on short, choppy sentences that can be revised to give the writing more grace and more smoothness. The revision will produce more clarity by showing the relationship between the important ideas.

These examples are from student essays. The first revision joins elements which were formerly separate and unrelated. This is only one way of rewriting the passage, and if you find you can improve on this way, please do.

1. My graduation was together. It was a nice feeling walking across that stage to get my diploma. This really showed me that I have an ability to accomplish my special goal which is nursing. It was fun being with my classmates for the last time. Graduation should be something to be proud of. It makes your parents feel good to know that you can do something in life besides jive around.

**Comment:** There are too many sentences beginning with "It" and "It was." The cause-effect relationship seems important here, but the writer does not make that clear. The revision below aims at helping to clarify the causal relationships in the passage.

**Revision:** My graduation was "together." It was a nice feeling walking across that stage to get my diploma because it showed me that I had the ability to go into nursing. It was also nice to be with my classmates for the last time. Graduation is something to be proud of because it makes your parents feel good to know that you can do something besides "jive around."

There are still problems in this passage. The sentence about being with classmates for the last time is not important to the discussion. (It also mistakenly implies that the writer is glad not to have to see her classmates again.) The writer also relies on one basic structure, the causal pattern beginning "because." This revision, however, keeps much of the original version while varying the length of the sentences.

Comment is provided after the next sample from a student composition. Revise the passage in the space provided to give it more variety of sentence length. Remember that there are several "right" ways of revising the passage. You may wish to see how others revise it.

2. The subject that I am about to write about is, I had one wish what would it be. I believe that I would wish for peace and mankind to come together. People all over the world should love everyone and the world will be better off.

**Comment:** Most of the first sentence is really unnecessary. The writer could simply state the subject, then offer his or her wish. The next two sentences should be joined together, and the last part of the second sentence, the wish that "mankind" "come together," could be included in the idea that people should love one another. These two sentences can be simplified a bit, then coordinated as independent clauses.

**Your revision:** _____

_____

_____

_____

_____

The next samples are also from student essays. Read each carefully, then fill in the box for comments. Spot the problems and suggest some solutions for the problems. Consider the kinds of structures the writer depends on and decide whether they are used well. Suggest what you think must be clarified if the passage is to be improved.

---

3. In "Little Dog" Mrs. Briggs' daughter is forced to stay with her all of the time. She never learned how to deal with society. Mrs. Briggs' daughter seemed to be a pet just as Mrs. Boyd's son Howard was to her. Mrs. Boyd never let Howard out of her sight even when he went away to college she soon followed.

---

**Your comment:** _____

_____

_____

_____

_____

_____

**Your revision:** _____

_____

_____

_____

_____

_____

---

4. What happens when justice depends on such things? Injustice. It hurts me to see such a beautiful thing as the idea of justice becoming, instead of truth, a matter of who you know and how much money you have. If this is happening, are the little people in this system to bear the foul air that this decaying system is creating?

---

**Your comment:** _____

_____

_____

_____

_____

**Your revision:** _____

_____

_____

_____

_____

_____

5. I think that "The Man Who Saw the Flood" was a very interesting story. I don't know if the meaning or the way the story seemed to me is correct, but it seemed to me that this is the point the author is trying to make: that most poor people never make their way out of poverty and hunger is because they don't want to. I'm not saying that all poor people, northern or southern think that way, but it was to my understanding, after reading this story that this is the way that one particular family was.

**Your comment:** _____

_____

_____

_____

_____

_____

**Your revision:** _____

_____

_____

_____

_____

_____

Discussing the passages in class may help clarify the problems each has. The "comment" sections are important for general discussion, since it helps to know how others see the problems any given passage has. If you are working alone, you may have a hard time seeing the difficulties of the passages. Try discussing them with someone else.

In the following sections, use passages taken from your own writing. If you have a hard time deciding which passages might be taken from your work and revised, ask your teacher or a classmate to choose some for you.

1.  **Your selection:** _____

_____

_____

_____

**Your comment:** _____

_____

_____

_____

_____

_____

_____

**Your revision:** _____

_____

_____

_____

2. **Your selection:** _____

_____

_____

_____

**Your comment:** _____

_____

_____

_____

**Your revision:** _____

_____

_____

_____

3.  **Your selection:** _____

_____

_____

_____

**Your comment:** _____

_____

_____

_____

**Your revision:** _____

_____

_____

_____

**4. Your selection:** _____

_____

_____

_____

**Your comment:** _____

_____

_____

_____

**Your revision:** _____

_____

_____

_____

**5. Your selection:** _____

_____

_____

_____

Your comment: _____

_____

Your revision: _____

_____

_____

# Varying Sentence Structure

Sometimes we write sentences without variety of length because we do not think about varying sentence structure. Using the same structure over and over gets boring. It can also prevent us from saying what we really mean. By using subordinate clauses and phrases more carefully, we can say exactly what we wish to. Everyone has had the experience of saying one thing but really meaning another. Control of sentence structure can avoid this. The main purpose of this section is to show how to vary sentence structure in your own writing. This section may also help you find bad habits in your writing that you can correct.

Use the following checklist of problems and solutions to the problems when you read the sample below. Use it, too, when you go over your own writing.

---

**CHECKLIST OF PROBLEMS**

1. *Starting every sentence with the subject of the independent clause*
   When you want to avoid this, begin with a participial phrase, infinitive phrase, or any of the subordinate clauses or phrases of time, place, and others we have discussed.
2. *Using the conjunction "and" in almost every sentence*
   Solve this problem simply. Find ways to subordinate a clause to your independent clause. Usually the conjunction "and" is not really working as a coordinate conjunction. When that is true, it is simple to decide how to subordinate part of the sentence.
3. *Habitual ways of starting sentences*
   Some writers always begin with "It is" or "There are" and cannot change their way. Solve this problem by seeing what your bad habits are and writing them on a card in front of you. Avoid them.

---

Examine the following passage from a student essay.

---

1. In this poem the poet is trying to get across a man's search for success. In the beginning the poet describes his never ending feeling that nothing is going right and his future looks dim. Until one day, his luck will change and he will accomplish something very worthwhile. Then, he will look to God and feel proud for the fact he has accomplished.

---

**Comment:** The writer uses beginnings of place and time too much. He or she starts with "In this poem," "In the beginning," "Until one day," and "Then." The writer is trying to get variety but did not notice that all the openings are pretty much the same. The sentences are about the same length. The first two sentences should be combined, and the last is not clear about what the "fact" is. Most of the beginning phrases are totally unnecessary for the sense of the passage, so they will be omitted in the revision below. Note that the revision aims at making the relationship between the major parts of the passage clearer.

> **Revision:** By describing his never-ending feeling that nothing is going right and that the future looks dim, the poet tells us about a man's search for success. One day, the poet says, the man's luck will change. Then he will look to God and feel proud of the fact he has accomplished something very worthwhile.

The next passage has many more problems than the first one. It has a number of choppy sentences and a number of unclear references. The causal relationship is never established. Because verbs are left out of independent clauses, several sentence fragments appear here. Yet the passage is very important. The writer clearly has something to say.

> 2. Life in the favela is tough, very tough. There isn't enough food and water as a matter of fact there isn't sufficient amounts of anything. With a great deal of hate and corruption. These people uneducated and unskilled. Places will not hire a single person who cannot read or write. The people have no money. And they have no friends except themselves. So this is why people must live in such a place as this. It just grows and grows until there are small sort of like cities of dirt, hunger, and prostitution.

**Comment:** It would seem that this was written very hastily. Ideas are repeated without real purpose or effect. Verbs are left out. Ideas are not really developed beyond a simple statement. The construction of result, or what ought to be the construction of result, does not seem to be clear. The author says, "So this is why...," but the fact is that we really do not know why "people must live in such a place as this." The writer has not told us. An analysis of the passage suggests that the reason they must live here is that they are uneducated and unskilled. Assuming this to be the case, we can offer a possible revision.

> **Revision:** Life in the favela is tough, very tough. There isn't a sufficient amount of food, water, or anything but hate and corruption. Businesses will not hire anyone who cannot read or write, and since these people are uneducated and unskilled, they can earn no money. Therefore they can live nowhere but in places like the favela, which grow and grow into cities of dirt, hunger, and prostitution.

The revision makes it clearer that the favela is a kind of slum that grows up in many places—probably near cities. In fact, the favela is the shantytown that often grows up near wealthy South American cities. The revision has kept as much of the original as possible, omitting only the detail about people in the favela having only one another for friends. If you feel this detail is important, perhaps you could do your own revision including it.

Study the next example carefully. Then study the comments which are made about it. When you feel you understand the comments, go on to do your own revision of the passage.

---

**Passage 1:** It all began one day in my Spanish class when my classmate was relating a strange incident that happened to her. Judy and her boyfriend, Nelson, were separated due to a vacation. Nelson left to go on a camping trip and decided to call Judy through his mind every night at the same time. He did so and each night Judy said she'd wake up all of a sudden without knowing why. When Nelson came back he asked Judy if anything odd happened to her. Judy told him about waking up every night and when they compared stories they found that she woke up around the same time he had concentrated on calling her through his mind.

---

**Comment:** In general this is not badly written, and many writers would leave it as it is. But we can see that some of the sentences could easily be combined by creating subordinate clauses of time, thereby clarifying some of those relationships. One of the time relationships that probably cannot be clarified is the first, "It all began. . ." In revising the passage, you will have to see if it can be included logically at all. Then, there is the further problem that most sentences begin with the simple subject. Something should be done to give a bit of variety to the passage. Remember that your purposes are to improve the passage, even if you do so only to a small degree.

**Your revision:** _____

_____

_____

_____

_____

_____

_____

_____

_____

Write both the comment and the revision for the next passages.

**Passage 2:** The highlight of the picnic was the food and getting ready to leave. It wasn't a rewarding experience for a freshman. It was disappointing, and useless. When the picnic was ending, I was overjoyed. Maybe in the future when another one is sponsored it would be much better. I wouldn't advise anyone to attend the most disastrous outing.

**Your comment:** _____

_____

_____

_____

_____

**Your revision:** _____

_____

_____

**Passage 3:** The second situation was when he was caught in the fruit market by a man and a woman who came in to buy some grapes. They assumed he worked there. They gave him the role of a worker in the store and to them he wasn't very important. He then became aware of the situation himself and just went along with the role they had given him. On another occasion, when he came out of the manhole, the people thought that he was a sewer worker. The people at the church gave him the role of a drunk who didn't know what he was doing. The policeman assumed that he was insane and was just going around making jokes. All of these incidents prove that society makes you, society tells you who you are and what position to take in life.

**Your comment:** _____

_____

_____

**Your revision:** _____

_____

_____

_____

_____

_____

_____

_____

Now, try the same exercise with two passages from your own writing. If necessary, ask your teacher to help you choose passages that need revision.

**Your first passage:** _____

_____

_____

_____

_____

_____

**Your comment:** _____

_____

_____

_____

_____

**Your revision:** _____

_____

_____

_____

_____

_____

**Your second passage:** _____

_____

_____

_____

_____

_____

**Your comment:** _____

_____

_____

_____

_____

_____

**Your revision:** _____

_____

_____

# strategies for achieving emphasis

# 1

# Emphasis: Parallel Structure

Emphasis is used as a way of keeping the reader's attention. It lets the reader know exactly what is most important, and it causes him or her to look closely at what you write. Some ways of producing emphasis can get tiring. For instance, always using an exclamation point can be very boring! Using a single sentence as a complete paragraph can work possibly once in an essay. After that it seems phony. Almost any technique used alone gets worn out pretty quickly. The techniques described in this section should all be used carefully. None should be used to extremes. The more of them you use, the more control you will have over the emphasis you get in your writing.

The purpose of writing ought to be to present information and careful opinions which have real value. Your writing should make that value plain to the reader. When you have a great deal of information and have worked up opinions you can defend, the emphasis of your writing can either help or hurt you in getting the ideas across. The best writing uses all the techniques mentioned in this section. But it uses them cautiously.

Probably the most important technique is parallel structure. It can be defined as using the same sentence pattern several times for effect. Parallel structure can also be identified as a repetition of words, structures, or whole sentences. However, the repetition must be controlled. It cannot be accidental.

The most famous example of parallel structure comes from the Latin of Julius Caesar. After he won a war against the enemy, he said:

> I came.   I saw.   I conquered.

Here three independent clauses of two words each become strong sentences. The three sentences, all with the same structure, follow one another quite naturally. The fact that they all have the same structure makes them special and it gives them a special feeling of importance. They could be equally strong in speech or in writing. This is such a simple, yet powerful, expression that it has become a model for parallel structure all over the world and in hundreds of languages. In its original language, Latin, it was just three words: *Veni. Vidi. Vici.* The repetition of the "v" sound (a "w" sound in Latin) at the beginning of each word made it an especially powerful statement. The repetition of "I" in the English version also helps emphasize the statement. Imagine if we were to translate it thus: "I came, saw, and conquered." It loses much in this form, yet it is a fairly accurate translation.

First are three examples of parallel sentences. The next three examples, 4, 5, and 6, offer parallel subordinate clauses. The next three present parallel predicates with completers, and the last three have parallel phrases. The parts that are parallel are boxed for identification.

1. | I am thoughtful. | You are cautious. | He is hesitant. |

2. | No one knew him. | No one saw him. | No one helped him. |

3. | Whoever wants him can have him. | Whoever gets him can keep him. |

4. | After we find the man, | after we secure his position, | and | after we give him the support he needs, | we may begin to see the results we hoped for.

5. | Because you waited patiently for this day to come, | and | because you deserve the kind of honor we know you have enjoyed in the past, | we want to show our own gratitude with this token of our appreciation.

6. We got what we wanted, but only | after we worked twenty years on the same job | and | after we saved every spare nickel, dime, and quarter we could find. |

7. The President | went where he wished, | did what he wished, | got what he wished. |

8. No one | had a better time, | or | had more friends, | or | had more fame | than Jasper.

9. I | ran upstairs, | threw open the window, | and | shouted the news to the world. |

10. | After breakfast, | after lunch, | and | after supper | he was sure to take a nap.

11. We didn't know if she was | next to you, | next to me, | or | next to Jasper. |

12. Julio was applauded | by his parents, | | by his teachers, | and

| by his friends. |

You will note that coordinating conjunctions join parallel subordinate clauses in examples 4, 5, and 6. Coordinating conjunctions also join predicates with completers in examples 8 and 9 and could have been used in example 7, where they are not necessary. Coordinating conjunctions also join the phrases in examples 10, 11, and 12.

Coordinating conjunctions join structures of equal value. Parallel construction uses structures of equal value, so you will find coordinating conjunctions important here. You may wish to review Section III, "Principles of Coordination."

Another important point to observe is the fact that the subordinate clauses often begin with the same subordinator when they are parallel. This is also true of the phrases. All the phrases in sentence 10 are phrases of time. Those in sentence 11 are phrases of place. The prepositional phrases in sentence 12 are called phrases of agency because they tell by what "agents" —that is, "doers"—Julio was applauded.

The rules to remember when using parallel structure are

---

1. Use the same sentence patterns or parts at least twice.
2. Use coordinating conjunctions to join clauses and phrases.
3. The same subordinators often can be used for parallel subordinate clauses and phrases. Sometimes different subordinators of the same kind (time, place) can be more effective in these constructions.

---

Keeping these rules in mind, offer some examples on your own of parallel structure. In each case follow the instructions by paralleling whole sentences, independent clauses, subordinate clauses, or phrases. Box the parallel structures.

**1. Parallel subordinate clauses:** _____

_____

_____

_____

_____

2. Parallel predicates with completers: _____

_____

_____

_____

3. Parallel sentences: _____

_____

_____

_____

4. Parallel phrases: _____

_____

_____

_____

## COMPOSITION POINTER

Look for an example of your recent writing where you might have used parallel structure but did not. Write that example in the first section below. Then rewrite it so that it uses the principle of parallel structure.

**Example from your own writing:** _____

_____

_____

_____

_____

_____

**Your revision, using parallel structure:** _____

_____

_____

_____

_____

# Emphasis: Choice of Words

Emphasis can be gained by using even a single word very carefully. The word that gets emphasis is usually either very technical or formal in nature. Or sometimes it can be colloquial or slangy. In either case the word that gets emphasis is going to come as a surprise to the reader. For that reason this method of achieving emphasis should be used carefully. Readers can handle only so many surprises before the novelty wears off.

Examine the next sentence. One word stands out as not being quite the same as the words surrounding it. The word is a slang word.

> We worked for months on the amendments and on the bill itself, until we learned that the President put the whammy on it.

The writer has controlled the choice of words so that we all understand the President did something bad. We do not even know what the bill was. Maybe it was to make the electric chair legal again. Maybe it was to force all citizens to be fingerprinted. We do not know. But we do know that from the writer's point of view the President did wrong. If the word "whammy" were any stronger, it might make us suspicious enough to look into the issue. As it is, we accept the writer's point of view.

The first four examples below use slang expressions in sentences that are fairly formal. The second four examples use a highly formal word in a relatively informal situation. In every case the word or words used for emphasis are boxed for identification. If you have the chance, discuss with a teacher or classmate why these words are emphatic.

1. We thought things would remain the same with Jasper as president, but, ⬚man,⬚ what a difference!

2. The director spent forty-five minutes telling us how we could find our way through the red tape, but what he said was a ⬚lot of baloney.⬚

3. Even though Rita was taking the entire affair much too seriously, we told her to ⬚hang in there⬚ and do her job.

4. At first Anita and Florry spoke very patiently with both of them, but soon Anita lost her temper and threatened to ⬚clobber⬚ them if they didn't leave.

5. Rita was not just mad at Benno. She was ⬚exasperated⬚ with him.

6. Luther was so still we thought he might have been in a state of suspended animation.

7. We all laughed, but Danielle chuckled in evil glee.

8. They got Chills. They got Danny. They got Simpson. But it was not until six months later that Phillips was apprehended.

---

**PUNCTUATION POINTER**

Most writers put quotation marks around a slang expression to show that they know the expression is not formal English. Sentence 3 above is often written this way: Even though Rita was taking the entire affair much too seriously, we told her to "hang in there" and do her job. Your teacher may wish you to use this technique in your own writing. Ask before you do the assignment below.

---

In the spaces below, write three sentences of your own in which you use slang words for emphasis. Then write three sentences in which you use highly formal words for emphasis.

1. _____

2. _____

3. _____

4. _____

5. _____

6. _____

# Emphasis: The Imperative and Direct Address

When you give your readers a direct command, you are using the imperative. Most writers use this form very little, but it can be very effective. The examples which follow are all simple imperatives. The word "you" usually does not appear in these sentences, but it is understood to be there in meaning.

1. Stop me if you've heard this one!
2. Don't change a thing!
3. Don't think for a second that Ralph Ellison is being funny here.
4. Take a good look at the social conditions around you.
5. Stay home unless you want to get hurt!
6. Keep your nose clean and everything will be all right.
7. Look closely at the imagery in this poem.
8. Try to imagine what would happen if you were in Hawaii.
9. Don't get any closer than you have to.
10. Hold still and say, "Cheese."

Write some examples of the imperative in the spaces below. Try to write sentences that you think could possibly be used in your own essays.

1. _____

2. _____

3. _____

4. _____

5. _____

6. _____

7. _____

8. _____

9. _____

10. _____


Direct address is somewhat like the imperative except it does not give an order. It singles out part of the audience and speaks directly to it. Or it singles out "you," the reader, and speaks to you. It is an example of writing which is addressed directly to a particular reader or group of readers. There is some overlap between the imperative and direct address, although the following examples do not give commands and so are not imperatives.

1. You women have made the entire society more sensitive to sex discrimination.
2. Why don't you see for yourself if Jasper really meant what he said.
3. Citizens, I want to warn you about tyranny.
4. My friends, you know how much the President wants to help you.
5. He has won this battle. He has won all the battles, but, Mr. Secretary, my day will come.
6. You know the kind of person Grant Montgomery was.
7. We all need to remember the first principles of democracy.
8. Let me address myself to the man in the street. Do you think for a moment the newspapers treat you fairly?
9. You can't tell a book by its cover.
10. Professor Jones, you can't imagine how I felt about the way that story ended.

Write your own examples of direct address below, aiming for as much variety as possible.


1. _____

2. _____

3. _____

4. _____

5. _____

6. _____

7. _____

8. _____

9. _____

10. _____

**Your revision using direct address or the imperative:** _____

_____

_____

_____

_____

# Emphasis: The Short-short Sentence

The extremely short sentence can be powerful for clinching a point or ending a discussion. It can hammer home the principal idea with force and conviction. But it will not work unless it is used sparingly. If it is overused, it simply looks like a gimmick and will convince nobody of your sincerity or concern.

The theory is simple enough: in the course of writing average-length sentences or even long sentences, try to condense your point in a sentence of no more than four or five words. The contrast is what usually takes the reader by surprise. One example is:

> When asked if I feel it is necessary for Congress to go to great lengths to ensure the doctrine of fairness in regard to the Executive offices and their constitutional prerogatives when under stress from either Congress or the Judiciary, I do not find myself inclined to ponder the question before offering an answer. It is, "No!"

This example is windy, of course, but it is windy in order to offer as much contrast as possible. The examples which follow are a bit more "normal" in character, though some of them may be a bit windy, too.

1. How often have people told Jasper that his style with women is essentially that of a male chauvinist? | Frequently! |

2. Miguel and Alonzo spent hours cruising the streets, checking the hangouts for a bit of female company. And after all that cruising they almost always took the old highway out to the drive-in movie and sneaked in through the back way with their lights out. | They were usually | alone. |

3. Ralph Ellison never writes about things that do not move him deeply or that will not move thousands of readers deeply. | He is involved. |

4. The space program has helped us catapult more than five hundred billion dollars' worth of hardware into the void where very few returns on the investment help any of the taxpayers who paid the bill. | Some | of us are getting angry. |

5. During the Second World War, one American general was caught behind German lines during the Battle of the Bulge. He was completely surrounded and his position looked hopeless, but when the German High Command offered him the chance to lay down his weapons and surrender his troops, he had a very simple answer. | "Nuts!" |

    In these examples the nature of the emphasis differs from sentence to sentence. The shorter the short-short sentence, the more emphatic the effect is likely to be, but the nature of the thought expressed in the sentence does a great deal to build emphasis. Since each of these short sentences follows (rather than precedes) a longer sentence, the effect is likely to be somewhat limited. Nonetheless, try constructing your own examples of this technique in the spaces below. You might go through some of your past writing looking for opportunities you missed for using the technique yourself.

1. _____

_____

_____

_____

2. _____

3. _____

4. _____

_____

_____

_____

_____

_____

5. _____

_____

_____

_____

_____

_____

# Emphasis: The Rhetorical Question

The rhetorical question has limited use, but it can be very effective. It is simply the posing of a question which either needs no answer or will be answered immediately in the text. What is a rhetorical question? It is illustrated in the preceding sentence. It is a question that needs no answer or that is answered by the writer. The question builds anticipation and suspense and makes readers more alert and watchful. They feel as if they are being spoken to directly.

Again, every writer must realize that it is easy to overdo the techniques that can produce emphasis in writing. And few techniques can be abused more easily than the rhetorical question, which is in many ways rather artificial and dramatic to begin with. So, with those words of caution, consider the following examples and give some thought to the possibility of using the technique in your own writing.

1. Who can believe the promises a politician makes? Who can trust a politician who does nothing but promise? Perhaps it is time to put an end to promises in American political life.
2. What is El Barrio? I'll tell you what El Barrio is to me.
3. Is there really a Santa Claus? Not for Little Jimmy the Fixer.
4. American literature is filled with tales of moral darkness. But what literature is not?
5. Do I have to fight your battles for you? Can't you stand up for yourself?
6. How much more of this political irresponsibility can America stand for?
7. Are we so blind that we cannot sympathize with Jasper?
8. What do the people in the streets say about the labor market? They say it will be a great day when we have full employment.
9. Give up? Not vote because things look dim? Never!
10. Why am I saying these things to you? It is because I have not given up on you.

---

**PUNCTUATION POINTER**

All questions, whether rhetorical or not, have the question mark (?) as the final mark of punctuation. In Spanish an upside down question mark comes first in a sentence to let the reader know he is reading a question. If we used Spanish punctuation we would make a question look like this: | ¿Are you all right? | English does not do this, so a question in English looks like this: | Are you all right? |

Follow the punctuation used in the examples above.

---

Write your own examples of rhetorical questions below.

1. _____

2. _____

3. _____

4. _____

5. _____

6. _____

7. _____

8. _____

9. _____

10. _____  _____

---

**COMPOSITION POINTER**

Find a passage in your recent writing where a rhetorical question or two might have been used but was not. Write the passage in the first section below. Then rewrite it in the second section using a rhetorical question for emphasis.


**Your writing sample:**   _____

_____

_____

_____

_____

_____

**Your revision using a rhetorical question:** _____

_____

_____

_____

_____

**6**

# Emphasis: Dialogue and Quotation

Dialogue is spoken language. People converse through dialogue. Most of our essay writing is different from spoken language because no one is giving us an instant response to what we say. For this reason we can sometimes give a great deal of emphasis to a piece of writing by representing a sentence or two as actual spoken dialogue. Doing this is not difficult. The only thing to remember is to put the sentence or sentences you write in quotation marks. The pattern for this would be:

" | Passage of dialogue. | "

---

**PUNCTUATION POINTER**

The sentence in dialogue begins with quotation marks, has a final point of punctuation, then has quotation marks to end the dialogue. If you add a question mark of your own or an exclamation point of your own which is not meant to be in the original dialogue, it comes outside the quotation marks. If the dialogue is itself a question or an exclamation, the quotation mark or the exclamation point goes inside the final quotation marks. Here are some examples:

Was it not General MacArthur who said, "I shall return"?

As General Grant said, "May I have your sword?"

---

A quotation is a piece of someone else's writing which you feel is important enough to include in your essay. It can range from a phrase all the way to twenty or thirty lines of type. One reason for using a quotation is to show that someone else agrees with your point or has said something that supports your view. Another reason may be to show that someone has not fully understood something and that you can help straighten it out. Often a good way to begin writing is to react to something another writer has said. There are two ways of using quotations, depending on how long they are. If the passage quoted is three lines long or shorter, run it directly into the text

so it looks like this, "  Passage quoted.  "

---

**PUNCTUATION POINTER**

When running the quotation into the main text, a comma comes first, then the quotation marks. The pattern is:

Your text + , + " + Passage quoted + . + "

---

When a passage quoted is longer than three lines, it is set off by indenting approximately three-quarters of an inch from the left and right in your text. Such quotations are single-spaced. They do not need quotation marks because setting them off in the text already identifies them as quotations. Usually a colon (:) is used to inform the reader that a quotation is coming, as in this example:

> This passage is an example of what a long quotation looks like or should look like in your essay. No quotation marks are necessary because of the indentation and single-spacing. Keep in mind that you have to give credit for using any quotation by telling your reader what author, book, and page you have used. This can be done either with a footnote such as the one at the bottom of this page, or with a reference in your text either before or after the quotation. Always check with your teacher first to see how it should be done.[1]

---

**PUNCTUATION POINTER**

The footnote number is always at the end of the passage. It is also always a little higher than the letter next to it, like this.[1] At the bottom of the page there should be a short line separating the quotation from the body of your writing, then the footnote number, still raised a half-space, as it is below.

---

[1]Lee A. Jacobus, *The Sentence Book* (New York: Harcourt Brace Jovanovich, 1976), p. 179.

The following list offers some examples of dialogue and quotation. The impact of the examples is limited because they appear alone and not in the middle of an essay, where they would be much more emphatic. Nonetheless, they are typical uses of the technique.

1. My Uncle Toby always said, "Jasper, don't ever get into politics!"

2. "Try to keep a cool head," I told the President.

3. "Why don't you think up something else?" asked Rita when she turned him down.

4. Sometimes I recall the words of Mark Twain: "If you don't like the weather in New England, wait a minute."

5. "Wait until next year." How many times have Dodger fans heard these words?

6. "No one is perfect," Heidi told her.

7. "Is this your opinion?" a student asked Ms. Hart.
   She turned and looked out the window. "I'm afraid so," she said.
   "Well, then," the student replied, "it looks as if you and I can't agree on how to handle this affair."
   "Maybe agreement is not necessary," she said.
   This is a conversation I overheard last week. I think it goes to show just how honest differences of opinion can be used to get things done.

8. D. H. Lawrence, in his essay on Edgar Allan Poe, says:

   > He is absolutely concerned with the disintegrating-processes of his own psyche. As we have said, the rhythm of American art-activity is dual.
   > 1. A disintegrating and sloughing of the old consciousness.
   > 2. The forming of a new consciousness underneath.[2]

9. "What about me? What about the man in the street?" Does Congress hear the pleas of the man in the street?

10. "Seek and ye shall find." This is the motto of the Star Detective Agency.

Example 7 above is important to look at because it shows a conversation between two people. The first person speaks in the first paragraph. Then, when the next speaker's dialogue is given, it is in a new paragraph, to show that the speaker has changed. The writer begins a new paragraph each time the speaker changes. This way it is clear to the reader that someone different is speaking.

---

[2]D. H. Lawrence, *Studies in Classic American Literature* (New York: Viking Press, 1971), p. 65.

Offer your own examples of dialogue in the spaces provided below. Try each of the models given above. If possible, find other ways of using dialogue and use those ways too.

1. _____

2. _____

3. _____

4. _____

5. _____

6. _____

7. _____

8. _____

9. _____

10. _____

# Emphasis: Punctuation

Probably the most familiar means of achieving emphasis is by using the exclamation point. It is not the only kind of punctuation that can be used for emphasis. Any punctuation that will set something off from the entire essay will contribute to emphasis. Any punctuation that is used rarely will also help achieve emphasis. The most important punctuation marks for achieving emphasis are:

1. ! The exclamation point, used in place of a period at the end of a sentence to indicate emphasis. Used in commands and to suggest alarm, fright, or fear.

2. : The colon, used to call attention to what follows. It stands for expressions like "such as" or "the following."

3. . . . The ellipsis, used to show that something is missing from the statement. Usually the missing element is understood by the reader. The ellipsis also is used in place of words or sentences left out of material you may quote.

4. — The dash, used to set off a part of the sentence. Unless the part—such as a clause or a phrase—comes at the end of the sentence, there are two dashes, as in the example in this sentence.

5. ( ) Parentheses. These are used in the same way as the dash (except that there must *always* be two parentheses). The parenthetical remark is an interruption of the sentence (sometimes right in the middle of the sentence) and needs no special punctuation other than the opening parenthesis and closing parenthesis, as shown in these examples.

6. [ ] Brackets show that the writer is explaining something that is somewhat apart from the general sentence. They are used inside a quotation or inside a parenthetical statement to indicate an interruption.

The following sentences use the punctuation marks discussed above. It is important to remember that using this kind of punctuation can get tiring. When you begin to try it in your own writing, be sure to use it sparingly.

1. Jasper and Rita won the election!
2. Don't give up the ship!
3. Give them a chance!
4. The institution had two kinds of criminals: the very clever and the insane.
5. He had only one purpose in mind: to become rich.
6. "One country. . . with. . . justice for all."
7. Were I to say what I really think—but no, I would regret it.
8. We hoist a flag (a big green one) to celebrate spring.
9. Some photographic chemicals (not the poisonous ones) have a pronounced odor.
10. Jasper—and everyone else from the Political Union—had some serious worries about Manny's candidacy.
11. "The writers of the Harlem Renaissance [like Langston Hughes] influenced American letters far more than they might have thought possible."

Use each variety of punctuation for emphasis yourself in the spaces provided below. Be prepared to explain what kind of emphasis you are developing here.

1. _____

2. _____

3. _____

4. _____

5. _____

6. _____

7. _____

8. _____

9. _____

10. _____

# tests
# and
# evaluations

Name _____ Date _____

# Pretest: Short Diagnostic Test.

Follow directions carefully.

**A. Subject and Predicate Verb** Each group of words below is missing either the subject or the predicate verb. Put a check mark in the subject column or the verb column to tell which one is missing.

Subject    Verb

_____    _____    1. Felipe under the covers so far from home and the comforts of family.
_____    _____    2. When heading out of town and turning past the old tower, was driving home.
_____    _____    3. Helen, who only wanted to be friends.
_____    _____    4. My old friend who never home.
_____    _____    5. The old casket with the green and speckled wallpaper all over its insides and the painted handles on its top next to the broken lock.

**B. The Sentence** Some of the following groups of words are sentences and some are not. Put a check mark next to each group of words that is a sentence.

Sentence

_____    1. Nearly driven insane, Alden managed to find his way out of the pit filled with snakes only to be driven blindly into the tiger's lair.

_____    2. Uncle James, managing so marvelously well now that Nanny's left.

_____    3. Speaking of terrifying incidents like the fall from the pantry stairs.

_____    4. You said it.

_____    5. Screaming, protesting, arguing, attacking, but definitely not crying in her beer.

187

_____   6. The beautiful Mable Hunter.

_____   7. An agreement between us is like a legal contract.

_____   8. Accepting this award would be the same as saying I was wrong.

_____   9. Crying out at the last minute before the accident.

_____   10. After the explanation, when everyone had cooled off a bit.

Write a complete sentence of your own:

_____

_____

**C. Agreement** Every verb must agree with its subject in number. If the subject is plural, then the verb must be plural. If the subject is singular, then the verb must be singular. Put a check mark next to each group of words in which the verb and subject are in agreement.

In agreement

_____   1. No friend of the family call me after dinner.

_____   2. Despite the Harveys, the Luannas, the Billy-Joes, no one has the right to look at me cross-eyed.

_____   3. If they annoys me I sticks my tongue out at them.

_____   4. My friend Eddie, who never asks anybody for anything, need a bit of help today.

_____   5. Because of the new law, Silly Otty got himself into more trouble than he thought possible.

_____   6. Like all the other people on my street, Billy Lassus, the kid with the gold tooth showing in his mouth, say he is as tough as holy hell.

**D. One-paragraph Essay** Write a tightly organized paragraph on one of the subjects below. Circle the number of the subject you choose.

1. The guys and girls I know have very different ideas about sex.
2. If there is another draft, women will be called to serve their country right along with the men.
3. The welfare system keeps people poor.
4. The U.S. will have to come to terms with Third World interests soon.
5. Supposedly, a college is an intellectual community.
6. If we all help each other, we will all do well. If we work against each other, we will hurt ourselves.
7. The U.S. cannot compete on a serious basis in Olympic sports.
8. One of the biggest "rip-offs" in the world is the price you have to pay for cosmetics.
9. Most guys I know are male chauvinists, but they won't admit it.
10. Birth control pills make women free and equal.

# Test: Section I. Basic Parts and Basic Problems.

**1. The Simple Subject**

A. In the list below, circle each word or phrase that can be the subject of a sentence.

|   |   |
|---|---|
| 1. porcupines | 11. Boy Scouts of America |
| 2. Reggie Jackson | 12. coolness |
| 3. from | 13. superior |
| 4. serve | 14. alarms |
| 5. imagination | 15. my Uncle Toby |
| 6. deliver | 16. being in a jam |
| 7. *Guinness Book of Records* | 17. pitted against Stalin |
| 8. although | 18. having read a book |
| 9. indirect | 19. surprised by fear |
| 10. silly | 20. signifying monkey |

B. In the spaces below, supply a list of words that can be subjects of a sentence.

1. _____     2. _____

3. _____     4. _____

5. _____     6. _____

7. _____     8. _____

9. _____     10. _____

11. _____    12. _____

13. _____    14. _____

15. _____    16. _____

17. _____    18. _____

19. _____    20. _____

Score: _____ (40 points maximum)

Name _____ Date _____

## 2. The Subject with Completers

A. Words that describe a simple subject help complete the meaning of the subject. The list below consists of simple subjects with completers that describe the subject. Put a circle around the words that are *not* the simple subject. Your circles will contain completers that describe the simple subject.

1. one unpleasant memory
2. my very best friend
3. someone's oldest shoe
4. Milwaukee's high scorer
5. starting again
6. Little Rita from Ontario
7. the next class
8. simple arithmetic
9. the song we heard
10. an active person

11. mean people indeed
12. sweet Elaine from next door
13. my humble beginnings
14. more than my earnings
15. his determination
16. Jasper's desire to vote
17. being absent from home
18. your final decision
19. a two-week vacation in Maine
20. love, like an old song

B. Supply reasonable completers for the subjects below. Add completers before and after the subject. Each of these counts as two points.

1. _____ intelligence _____

2. _____ activities _____

3. _____ Juarez _____

4. _____ Luther Hamilton _____

5. _____ Standard Oil Company _____

6. _____ talent _____

7. _____ difficulty _____

8. _____ shame _____

9. _____ screens _____

10. _____ calls _____

Score: _____ (40 points maximum)

### 3. The Simple Predicate

A. The simple predicate is a verb whose action is complete. It can be the verb of a sentence. Put a circle around the words in the list below which by themselves can be verbs in a sentence.

| | |
|---|---|
| 1. decide | 11. Jerry |
| 2. intended | 12. style |
| 3. place | 13. dripping |
| 4. alarming | 14. sleep |
| 5. standing | 15. did not lie |
| 6. having put | 16. was trying |
| 7. would have said | 17. will be sick |
| 8. might | 18. calling |
| 9. having begun | 19. shove |
| 10. grasp | 20. seashore |

B. Write twenty words below which can be verbs in a sentence. Do not use any from the list above.

1. _____  2. _____

3. _____  4. _____

5. _____  6. _____

7. _____  8. _____

9. _____  10. _____

11. _____  12. _____

13. _____  14. _____

15. _____    16. _____

17. _____    18. _____

19. _____    20. _____

Score: _____ (40 points maximum)

Name _____ Date _____

## 4. The Predicate with Adverb Completers

A. Adverb completers give information about how something is done. They are not verbs themselves but they describe the action of verbs. Circle the words in the list below which are adverb completers. Do not circle the verb or helper verb (such as "was" or "have").

1. voted now
2. soon wrote again
3. now prescribed for her
4. would never tell
5. saw from a distance
6. explained once
7. noticed right away
8. sees far ahead of her
9. remains totally silent
10. sounds crazy to me
11. fell on his prat
12. after having said
13. work now, play later
14. carefully designed by Leo
15. approached with serious intent
16. regarded hopefully
17. suddenly stopped short
18. never described before
19. looked up again
20. beautifully shot that time

B. In the spaces below write a good predicate verb with adverb completers. You may put the completer before, after, or between the parts of the verb.

1. _____    2. _____

3. _____    4. _____

5. _____    6. _____

7. _____    8. _____

9. _____    10. _____

11. _____    12. _____

13. _____    14. _____

15. _____  16. _____

17. _____  18. _____

19. _____  20. _____

Score: _____ (40 points maximum)

## 5. The Sentence Fragment

A. A sentence fragment is only part of a sentence. It is not a complete thought and cannot stand by itself as a sentence. In the list below, check which are fragments and which are sentences.

Sentence   Fragment

1. My Uncle Toby, almost fifty years old now. ☐ ☐
2. No one is here. ☐ ☐
3. They all from the sovereign state of New York. ☐ ☐
4. Let us start over again. ☐ ☐
5. After having one more chance. ☐ ☐
6. When we had everything in our favor. ☐ ☐
7. Because you tried too hard. ☐ ☐
8. No one thought of that. ☐ ☐
9. Being much too overtired for another swim now. ☐ ☐
10. Simply wanting the basics: housing and meals. ☐ ☐
11. After having made all the arrangements we needed. ☐ ☐
12. By insisting on our promptness. ☐ ☐
13. When should we go to town? ☐ ☐
14. Are you being careful enough for Juan? ☐ ☐
15. My mother near the place where we used to hang out. ☐ ☐
16. A photograph of four people. ☐ ☐
17. My friend, Margaret Minturno, from the hospital. ☐ ☐
18. Benito who everyone thought was great. ☐ ☐
19. We left after insisting that Jasper and Rita pay. ☐ ☐
20. Anything like this possible again? ☐ ☐

B. Decide which of the examples on the other side of the page are fragments. Show whether they need a subject or a predicate verb to make them into sentences. Some may need both. Some may be complete sentences; for those, do not put a check mark.

1. My Uncle Toby from Argentina, near Brazil.  ☐ ☐

2. After a little while.  ☐ ☐

3. Manno sensing trouble.  ☐ ☐

4. Despite our pleas, he left.  ☐ ☐

5. The table which we put in the outer lobby.  ☐ ☐

6. Where no one else was.  ☐ ☐

7. Have you got everything ready?  ☐ ☐

8. On account of the party the other day.  ☐ ☐

9. When people think they have it made.  ☐ ☐

10. Alma in the garage with the motor.  ☐ ☐

11. The picture of all of us laughing at the joke.  ☐ ☐

12. Fred being as cute as he could.  ☐ ☐

13. We all in big trouble now.  ☐ ☐

14. We tried everything we could.  ☐ ☐

15. Rita Moreno used to be in the movies.  ☐ ☐

16. After Luther, the only person who could.  ☐ ☐

17. Striking out for a brand-new place to set up camp.  ☐ ☐

18. All of us bothered by his yapping.  ☐ ☐

19. My sweetheart really likes me.  ☐ ☐

20. Yes, a very heavy subject.  ☐ ☐

Score: _____ (40 points maximum)

## 6. The Run-on Sentence

A. Many of the sentences below are run-on. Some are fused sentences—no punctuation at all. Some are comma splices—with a comma in place of a semicolon or a period. Decide which they are and correct them with the proper punctuation. Do not forget to capitalize the first letter of any new sentence you create. Each question counts as two points.

1. After José went to the movies, he spent his money as he wished.
2. My Uncle Toby had big feet his shoe size was close to 14.
3. Half the class was bored, half the class was excited.
4. We all had to pitch in and help no one else would do it for us.
5. Since everyone tried to do the job right, it got done very quickly.
6. Rita never said a word about it, Jasper certainly would not mention it, either.
7. Until we were sure what we were doing, Zaida held her ground, she wanted to be as sure of herself as possible.
8. Felipe, who had such a silvery tongue, was the first to speak, he convinced everyone that there was still hope for the project.
9. The plant that Mitchell referred to had only one smokestack for each of the blast furnaces, so its capacity was fairly limited.
10. Most of us say what we mean, but sometimes we hedge a bit so as not to hurt a person's feelings.

B. Another kind of run-on sentence is the overloaded sentence. It is characterized by too many details or by more information than one sentence can handle. In the following overloaded sentences, put a box around the material that could be left out of the sentence and saved for a new sentence. Each question counts as two points.

1. No one knows how I can keep going the way I do, year after year, up until all hours, even in the summertime when other people get some rest that they need.
2. Jasper spoke eloquently about the way elections should be conducted in colleges where political science has an effect on everyday life for every student who has an interest in campus affairs of the kind that he is interested in.

3. Because of the nature of the meeting, and because no one wanted to hurt Rita's feelings, everyone tried to soft-pedal the criticism that probably should have been leveled against her, given the circumstances of the outburst that stopped the whole show when Rita said she could not stand to sit there any more with what was going on.

4. Some parts of New York seem to be falling down or burning up with all kinds of goings-on scaring residents each day when they hear the bells ringing from the fire engines or the police cars, even late at night and early in the morning.

5. The kind of medical help you can expect in an emergency is likely to be efficient and good the way it was when Helen stumbled into the fan when she broke her finger and people thought the blood was coming from her face and the doctor calmed the whole office in no time.

C. In the spaces below, rewrite sentences 1 through 5 above, to solve the problems of overloading and/or the problems of repetition and unnecessary information.

1. _____

_____

_____

_____

_____

2. _____

_____

_____

_____

3. _____

_____

_____

_____

_____

_____

4. _____

_____

_____

_____

_____

_____

5. _____

_____

_____

_____

_____

_____

Score: _____ (40 points maximum)

Name _____ Date _____

## 7. Subject and Predicate Agreement

A. Every subject must agree with its predicate verb. If the subject is singular (referring to only one thing), the verb must be singular. If the subject is plural (referring to more than one thing), the predicate verb must be plural. In the following list, circle the examples which have the verb in agreement with the subject.

1. Toby want to go with me.
2. The distance were great.
3. Nobody know who I am.
4. People have no fun.
5. I had some trouble.
6. He scream at me.
7. The children was well behaved.
8. You was quiet enough.
9. We were together at last.
10. Sam was alarmed.
11. Were Janice stung?
12. Do Julio play guitar?
13. Have Constance gone?
14. Are you ready?
15. What comments have you made?
16. Where is the packages?
17. Jasper were very weird.
18. Do this hurt?
19. The corpse were found.
20. No one are at home.

B. Decide if the sentences below have their subjects and predicate verbs in agreement. If they do, mark them either singular or plural.

|  | Singular | Plural |
|---|---|---|
| 1. Marco, Hammer, and Jim saw me. | ☐ | ☐ |
| 2. Everyone is here. | ☐ | ☐ |
| 3. My people want food. | ☐ | ☐ |
| 4. Have we made a decision? | ☐ | ☐ |
| 5. Are you calm now? | ☐ | ☐ |
| 6. The Yankees may win the pennant. | ☐ | ☐ |
| 7. Someone has my watch. | ☐ | ☐ |
| 8. The class has planned a party. | ☐ | ☐ |
| 9. Now I am depressed. | ☐ | ☐ |
| 10. Accents are interesting. | ☐ | ☐ |

C. In the spaces provided below, write your own subject and predicate verb. Keep them in agreement. Show whether they are singular or plural.

|  | Singular | Plural |
|---|---|---|
| 1. _____ | ☐ | ☐ |
| 2. _____ | ☐ | ☐ |
| 3. _____ | ☐ | ☐ |
| 4. _____ | ☐ | ☐ |
| 5. _____ | ☐ | ☐ |
| 6. _____ | ☐ | ☐ |
| 7. _____ | ☐ | ☐ |
| 8. _____ | ☐ | ☐ |
| 9. _____ | ☐ | ☐ |
| 10. _____ | ☐ | ☐ |

Score: _____ (40 points maximum)

### 8. Pronoun Agreement

A. Pronouns must agree in number and gender with the word or words they refer to. In the sentences below, underline the proper form of the pronoun in order to make it agree with its referent.

1. Everybody in the women's lounge had (their/her) eyes focused on the picture.
2. Eduardo and I had (our/their) attention drawn to the disturbance.
3. The Portland family put (its/their) trash out on the street.
4. The people want (their/its) safety put uppermost.
5. The United Nations heard (itself/themselves) praised mightily.
6. Everyone I saw at the fraternity meeting gave (his/their) okay to the proposal.
7. Clumsiness is (their/its) own reward.
8. A good idea has (its/one's) place in every get-together we have.
9. The committeewoman decided that (they/she) would call a meeting at once.
10. Florence told us after the meeting was finished that (it/she) voted against the motion.
11. The entire assembly settled (itselves/itself) with an audible rumble.
12. Moore's photographic team had (itself/themselves) photographed on top of the mountain.
13. The Chord-o-liers, who had six gold and four platinum records in succession, could not get (their/his) tone-quality together.
14. The basketfuls of fruit had (its/their) handles decorated in the same colors.
15. One of the girls mentioned (their/her) own name early in the evening.
16. Strange, but none of (us/ourselves) knew my name in the play.
17. Friends do not like to hear (oneself/themselves) spoken of in a slighting fashion.
18. He has tonsilitis, but (it is/they are) not catching.
19. Sharon is one of those girls who like to have (her/their) cake and eat it too.

20. The main body of the population will complain, but (it/they) will eventually pay the tax.

B. The following sentences have blanks where pronouns should be. For each sentence choose an appropriate pronoun from the list below, and write it in the blank so as to make good sense of the sentence. The list to choose from is: which, that, one, who, it, its, each, their, all, everybody, themselves, itself, himself, herself, any, his, her, one's, someone.

1. She was one of the women _____ protested most vigorously.

2. My Uncle Toby had _____ shoes scratched by the dog.

3. This is something _____ I wanted to talk to you about.

4. Sharon is someone _____ does not permit

_____ own ideas to be taken lightly.

5. _____ at the convention wanted _____

candidate to win.

6. Fred watered_____ of Jasper's plants while he was away.

7. Susan and Hilda would not give _____ of

_____ secrets to the cooks in the dormitory.

8. Only one of my girlfriends ever lost _____ purse in the subway.

9. Luther thought of _____ as _____ of the most handsome men in town.

10. Dujardin was grateful to _____ friend Joyce.

11. None of the survivors could even say _____ own name.

12. _____ name is one's treasure.

13. The turtle protected _____ by rolling over on

_____ back.

14. Didn't he give you _____ of his ice cream?

15. Is this the road _____ gave you so much trouble when you went to Buffalo?

# Test: Section II. Constructing Clauses and Phrases.

### 1. The Independent Clause

A. The independent clause has a subject and a predicate; it can stand alone as a sentence. Check the box next to each independent clause below.

Independent
Clause

1. Margarita and her cousins from Hawaii. ☐

2. Seeing as how we were struggling. ☐

3. Jasper voted Democratic. ☐

4. This tire outlasted the others. ☐

5. We found our friends. ☐

6. Marilyn from California. ☐

7. We have no business being here. ☐

8. Combined with everything else today. ☐

9. Struck like greased lightning. ☐

10. After having my car overhauled. ☐

11. When we try out our motorcycle. ☐

12. The bakery next to our house. ☐

13. Philadelphia, here I come. ☐

14. Where we saw Federico sitting. ☐

15. In the way I used to do. ☐

16. When will we go home? ☐

17. The idea was really not so good. ☐

18. If I can begin again. ☐

19. Which one is mine? ☐

20. During the time it takes to bring me home. ☐

B. In the spaces provided, write brief independent clauses. Try not to repeat any of those above. Each item counts as two points.

1. _____

2. _____

3. _____

4. _____

5. _____

6. _____

7. _____

8. _____

9. _____

10. _____

Score: _____ (40 points maximum)

Name _____ Date _____

## 2. The Subordinate Clause

A. The subordinate clause contains a subject and a predicate verb. However, it cannot stand alone as a sentence. It needs another clause to complete its sense. Circle each subordinate clause in the list below.

1. My Uncle Toby
2. After being engaged
3. Until you wept
4. Then he said
5. Nobody had a dime
6. Expecting nothing more
7. Winking is silly
8. Designing houses
9. Every single non-detergent soap
10. Without a doubt

11. Until James said what he did
12. Tell us what happened
13. Larger than a Russian wolfhound
14. Even if Freddy told me himself
15. Unless the President says so
16. Willing to have me over
17. Since no one else could go
18. Precision helps
19. While everybody slept
20. Near where we used to eat

B. Write your own subordinate clauses below. Try to get as much variety into them as possible. Each item counts as two points.

1. _____

2. _____

3. _____

4. _____

5. _____

6. _____

7. _____

8. _____

9. _____

10. _____

### 3. The Participial Phrase

A. Participial phrases in the present tense sometimes start with an "-ing" form of the verb. In the past tense, participial phrases sometimes start with the "-ed," "-en," or irregular form of the verb. These forms are called participles. They are not predicate verbs even though they have a resemblance to them. Participial phrases can also begin with subordinators like "after" and "until." Identify the participial phrases below by circling them.

1. Trying again
2. Caught by Jasper
3. Relenting once more
4. Deciding against my will
5. Enjoying myself
6. Responding to treatment
7. Before going away
8. Nearly signing the treaty
9. In singing school
10. Even after my speech
11. When buying a new toaster
12. Offending the brother
13. Collopy was hurting himself
14. Brought down by hatred
15. Approved by the President himself
16. When asked by the press
17. Minding the store
18. Nursing is my life
19. Not having a thing to do
20. Living near me

B. Write your own examples of participial phrases in the spaces below. Try to get as much variety into them as possible. Each item counts as two points.

1. _____

2. _____

3. _____

4. _____

5. _____

6. _____

7. _____

8. _____

9. _____

10. _____

Score: _____ (40 points maximum)

**4. The Prepositional Phrase**

A. The prepositional phrase consists of a preposition followed by the name of something. Any preposition, such as "to," "of," and "in," can begin a prepositional phrase. Identify the prepositional phrases below by circling them.

1. in my solitude
2. with my friend Jim
3. after you left
4. behind my barn
5. to heaven and back
6. disguising Jasper
7. from my buddy
8. to male chauvinism
9. up in Michigan
10. at my expense

11. for you alone
12. while I snored
13. when you called
14. why not write
15. see me later
16. do something
17. be patient today
18. within the time set aside
19. from hunger
20. for the birds

B. Write your own prepositional phrases in the spaces below. Each item counts as two points.

1. _____

2. _____

3. _____

4. _____

5. _____

6. _____

7. _____

8. _____

9. _____

10. _____

Score: _____ (40 points maximum)

## 5. The Infinitive Phrase

A. The infinitive phrase usually begins with the infinitive form of the verb, such as "to be," "to have," "to pass," "to kick," "to run." It often has completers which name something. Put a circle around each infinitive phrase below.

|     |                          |     |                       |
|-----|--------------------------|-----|-----------------------|
| 1.  | to be or not to be       | 11. | to avoid involvement  |
| 2.  | to sing my song          | 12. | to take my picture    |
| 3.  | to be defined by sex     | 13. | to heaven             |
| 4.  | to here and back         | 14. | to see Rita           |
| 5.  | to you, my love          | 15. | to elaborate on that  |
| 6.  | to defend with my life   | 16. | to smell a rat        |
| 7.  | to see you leave         | 17. | to pass out           |
| 8.  | to all of us             | 18. | to him who passes     |
| 9.  | to begin the meeting     | 19. | not to be offended    |
| 10. | to mean what we say      | 20. | to see through it     |

B. Write your own infinitive phrases in the spaces below. Each item is worth two points.

1. _____

2. _____

3. _____

4. _____

5. _____

6. _____

7. _____

8. _____

9. _____

10. _____

Score: _____ (40 points maximum)

# index

*Only the most important problem areas are identified
in this index. It is intended to be an aid to student and instructor
for purposes of review or for dealing with specific problems.*

A 6
B 7
C 8
D 9
E 0
F 1
G 2
H 3
I 4
J 5